SINGLE
BUT NOT ALONE

DIANE SIMS

A STRANG COMPANY

SINGLE, BUT NOT ALONE by Diane Sims
Published by Creation House
A Strang Company
600 Rinehart Road
Lake Mary, Florida 32746
www.creationhouse.com

This book or parts thereof may not be reproduced in any form, stored in a retrieval system, or transmitted in any form by any means—electronic, mechanical, photocopy, recording, or otherwise—without prior written permission of the publisher, except as provided by United States of America copyright law.

Unless otherwise noted, all Scripture quotations are from the New American Standard Bible Updated Edition, Copyright © 1960, 1962, 1963, 1968, 1971, 1972, 1973, 1975, 1977, 1995 by The Lockman Foundation. Used by permission. www.Lockman.org

Scripture quotations marked AMP are from the Amplified Bible. Old Testament copyright 1965, 1987 by the Zondervan Corporation. The Amplified New Testament copyright © 1954, 1958, 1987 by the Lockman Foundation. Used by permission.

Scripture quotations marked NAS are from the New American Standard Bible, Copyright © 1960, 1962, 1963, 1968, 1971, 1972, 1973, 1975, 1977 by The Lockman Foundation. Used by permission. www.Lockman.org

Scripture quotations marked NIV are from the Holy Bible, New International Version. Copyright © 1973, 1978, 1984, International Bible Society. Used by permission.

Scripture quotations marked KJV are from the King James Version of the Bible.

Cover design by Rafael Sabino

Copyright © 2004 by Diane Sims
All rights reserved

Library of Congress Control Number: 2004114754
International Standard Book Number: 1-59185-721-X

05 06 07 08 — 98765432
Printed in the United States of America

To my parents, the late Ozie and Dorothy Sims, who instilled the strong Christian values that guide my life daily. I am so thankful to be your daughter. As your youngest of twelve, your baby girl has found her destiny in Christ. Through it all, I have learned to trust in God.

Acknowledgments

A SPECIAL THANKS TO my sister and best friend, Marquetta Sims-Berry, who always told me I could. You were always there to listen and care. You were right all along.

Thank you, Darlene Celise Scott, my sister, for your support of this project.

Thanks to my niece, Sherri Carter, for your excitement and motivation.

My gratitude to the rest of my family; your ongoing encouragement has brought me great joy. I thank God for such strong family ties. I am able to be who I am because of you.

Thanks to my spiritual mother, Maureen Lee, for your prayers in birthing this miracle.

A warm thank you to Susan Owens for your time and encouragement.

Finally, thank you to everyone at Creation House for joining me in this powerful endeavor.

Contents

Introduction	1
1 Reality Check	3
2 The Don'ts in a Relationship	13
3 As She Waits	33
4 From Pain to Purpose	49
5 Arise, My Daughter	57
6 Unfading Beauty	67
7 Tunnel Vision	81
8 Strength in Turmoil	93
9 Courage Above Defeat	107
10 From Rags to Riches	119
Epilogue	132

Introduction

What is the true meaning of single? What usually comes to mind when you think of single? Do you think of single in comparison to a pair, one instead of two? Do you think of incompleteness rather than completeness? Do you think of brokenness rather than wholeness?

On the other hand, do you allow others to define what single is for you? Do you feel insecure as a single woman? Are your thoughts about singleness positive or negative? How do you view yourself as a single woman?

It is important for single women to identify their own perception of what being single means in order to maximize their personal gifts. This is because Jesus desires to utilize you as a purified vessel for His anointing to flow through. However, a negative self-perception can limit His presence in your life. Regardless of what the cause may appear to be on the surface, a negative self-perception results from not understanding and accepting God's true love for you.

The magnitude of Christ's love for you goes far beyond any imaginable measure. His love breaks strongholds, heals, and delivers. Many single women have suffered from heartbreaks, rejection, abandonment, abuse, and loneliness. As a result, those painful experiences have engulfed the concept of what being single means to them. Being a single woman does not define who you are. Who you are in Christ defines who you are.

You must realize that singleness can be a means to an end, and not the end to any means. As you already well know, life is truly a journey. You will encounter many smooth and bumpy roads. However, be of good cheer! God uses these experiences for your benefit to purify and strengthen you. Your present circumstances will not last forever. Paul states in Romans 8:18, "For I consider that the sufferings of this present time are not worthy to be compared with the glory that is to be revealed to us."

Being single is part of this journey as God prepares you for marriage. God loves women too much to give them away prematurely in marriage. You are a joint heir with Christ. You have been adopted as a daughter of God through Jesus Christ. God is your father. Like any father, He is not too quick to give away His daughters that He highly values as rare precious jewels.

Now, let us define the single woman from God's perspective. She is an unmarried woman on a journey in preparation for God's divine plan in operation in her life. Preparation does not imply the presence of loneliness, despair, unhappiness, or depression. Preparation simply involves getting ready for something in advance. Remember that God is in control. He is preparing you for something great. It is my prayer that as you read this book, God will reveal His plan and purpose for your life. As a result, you will experience the presence of His overempowering love that reassures you that you are never alone.

CHAPTER 1

Reality Check

WOMEN HAVE COME a long way in this society in being recognized as equal to their male counterparts. Women have gone to space, lead multibillion dollar corporations, and ruled in courtrooms. In today's society, it has been perhaps subconsciously ingrained into the minds of women that they can do whatever they want. Women have been taught that they no longer need men to survive. After all, they have been taught they can do whatever men can do, as well or better.

As a result women have excelled in sports, entertainment, and politics. I am thankful to the strong women that dedicated and risked their lives on the frontlines fighting for what women have today. These courageous women should not be forgotten. However, you need to recognize that all blessings come from God, your Father.

The closer you walk with God, the more it becomes evident how great He is and how small and powerless you are without Him. The reality is you can do nothing without Him. As Philippians 4:13 reads, "I can do all things through Him who strengthens me." These things cannot be accomplished without His supernatural strength. If you depend on your own strength, you will become weary.

I recently took a beginner's bowling class. The instructor had many years of experience. He had bowled on several champion leagues throughout the country. In other words, he was a seasoned bowler. He was well qualified to teach this course.

On the first day of class, he laid out the rules of conduct for this class. Most people at bowling alleys eat food, drink soda, and socialize, right? Well, because this was a formal class, we were expected to act accordingly. Therefore, food, excessive socializing, and personal phone calls were prohibited during class time.

We learned proper body mechanics and technique to smoothly roll the bowling ball down the lane. As you carry the ball and extend it forward, the weight of the ball will gently extend itself backward. The ball can then be effortlessly rolled down the lane.

I had a problem in this area. I was carrying the weight of the bowling ball without allowing the ball to extend itself back. I would then force the ball down the lane, straining my arm muscles. This exhausted me and left my arm very sore.

Week after week I kept making the same mistake, overworking. I was using my own strength to force the ball to do what it could otherwise do alone without my effort. I arrived to the conclusion that I could do better if I would just follow the teacher's instructions. The reality was that his way was better than my way. After following his instructions, this game became quite enjoyable for me.

God revealed to me some valuable realities from this experience. First of all, just as there were "rules of conduct" involved in what seemed to be a simple bowling class, so God has created laws and commandments for us to follow in order to excel

Reality Check

in His Kingdom. He sent His own beloved Son to earth to demonstrate His commandments in practice. In obedience to His father, Jesus died on the cross and became the blood sacrifice for every sin and iniquity. As Isaiah 53:4–5 (KJV) states: "Surely he hath borne our griefs, and carried our sorrows: yet we did esteem him stricken, smitten of God, and afflicted. But he was wounded for our transgression, he was bruised for our iniquities: the chastisement of our peace was upon him; and with his stripes we are healed." Wow, what a qualified teacher He is! Yes, Jesus is your Master and Teacher.

As you walk with Him, He continually directs and shelters you in His arms. He carries your heavy load so that you do not have to. He can only carry it if you surrender it over to Him. Jesus says in Matthew 11:28–30 (KJV), "Come unto me, all ye that labour and are heavy laden, and I will give you rest. Take my yoke upon you, and learn of me; for I am meek and lowly in heart: and ye shall find rest unto your souls. For my yoke is easy, and my burden is light." Oh, how restful it is when you stop overworking and attempting to control your burdens and just yield to the Master's instructions.

Women bear unnecessary pains and struggles by doing things their way to control their own lives, determine their own future, and create their own destiny without God. In the Bible, Sarah demonstrates how using your own efforts to control your destiny lead to disaster and turmoil. God told Abraham that Sarah, his wife, would have a son and his offspring would be as numerous as the stars in the sky. "And he brought him outside [his tent into the starlight] and said, Look now toward the heavens and count the stars—if you are able to number them. Then He said to him, so shall your descendants be" (Gen 15:5, AMP). However, Sarah grew tired of waiting and decided to take matters into her hands. Let us read:

> And Sarai said to Abram, See here, the LORD has restrained me from bearing [children]. I am asking you

> to have intercourse with my maid; it may be that I can obtain children by her. And Abram listened to and heeded what Sarai said. So Sarai, Abram's wife, took Hagar her Egyptian maid, after Abram had dwelt ten years in the land of Canaan, and gave her to her husband Abram to be his [secondary] wife. And he had intercourse with Hagar, and she became pregnant; and when she saw that she was with child, she looked with contempt upon her mistress and despised her. Then, Sarai said to Abram, May [the responsibility for] my wrong and deprivation of rights be upon you! I gave my maid into your bosom, and when she saw that she was with child, I was contemptible and despised in her eyes. May the LORD be the judge between you and me. But Abram said to Sarai, See here, your maid is in your hands and power; do as you please with her. And when Sarai dealt severely with her, humbling and afflicting her, she [Hagar] fled from her.
> —GENESIS 16:2–6, AMP

It seemed rational to Sarah to speed up the process "helping God" fulfill his plan by using her own means. However, there is a harsh reality to carrying your own weight. The entire weight of it rests on you as well as the additional weight that it magnetically attracts. It produces a rebound effect. Sarah saw Hagar as an opportunity to have the child that she had always longed for. Too often, women look to other women for their blessing.

They do not think that God will bless them personally, so they look to other women who appear to have what they want. They begin acting like them, dressing like them, and talking like them, in hopes of receiving their own miracle. They look to other women for the direction that only God can give. As Sarah gave her husband to Hagar, so do many women give up their hopes, dreams, and talents, trying to become like someone else. Perhaps Sarah took matters into her own hands because she was trying to protect God just

Reality Check

in case He did not fulfill His promise. After all, who would be left to depend on if the Almighty God let her down? Who would she turn to then?

Have you ever had similar thoughts? Although you may think you are protecting God, you are actually yielding to fear and doubt. God's Word and promises are true. He does not need for you to attempt to bring them to pass. Nor does he need you doubting His word in fear that if He does not fulfill His promise, then you will have no hope. The reality is that God is your shield and protector. You are not His. My sister, when God gives you a vision, speaks a word to you, or sends you a promise, it will surely come to pass. It has to come to pass. This same God created the heaven and the earth by His spoken word. God's promises have more validity and truth than what any human being could ever attempt to promise you.

Once Sarah had accomplished her goal, everything suddenly backfired on her. When Hagar found out that she was pregnant, she became resentful and despised Sarah. Blessings cannot be birthed when you have tried to create them yourself. You can only create substitutes that birth turmoil, strife, and destruction. This brings damage to yourself and to others whom you have manipulated. The Spirit of God births blessings with perfection and completion as He did with the Virgin Mary.

Let us read:

> And in the sixth month the angel Gabriel was sent from God unto a city of Galilee, named Nazareth, To a virgin espoused to a man whose name was Joseph, of the house of David; and the virgin's name was Mary. And the angel came in unto her, and said Hail, thou that art highly favored, the LORD is with thee: blessed art thou among women. And when she saw him, she was troubled at his saying, and cast in her mind what manner of salutation this should be. And the angel said unto her, Fear not, Mary: thou hast found favor with God. And behold thou shall conceive in thy womb, and bring forth a son, and

shalt call his name JESUS. He shall be great, and shall be called the Son of the Highest: and the Lord God shall give unto him the throne of his father David: And he shall reign over the house of Jacob forever; and of his kingdom there shall be no end. Then said Mary unto the angel, How shall this be, seeing I know not a man? And the angel answered and said unto her, The Holy Ghost shall come upon thee, and the power of the Highest shall overshadow thee: therefore also that holy thing which shall be born of thee shall be called the Son of God. And, behold, thy cousin Elisabeth, she hath also conceived a son in her old age: and this is the sixth month with her, who was called barren.

—Luke 1:26–36, kjv

What a powerful encounter. God directly revealed to Mary, through the angel Gabriel, her divine destiny. When she saw the angel she was troubled. I believe she was overtaken by amazement. Has God given you a revelation or foreshadowing of your destination? Has He delivered His divine purpose for you into your spirit in such a powerful magnitude that your mind could not process it? Ephesians 3:20 (kjv) states, "Now unto him that is able to do exceeding abundantly above all that we ask or think, according to the power that worketh in us." If God has a blessing in store for you, then get ready, my sister! It will be on the way before long.

The angel told Mary not to fear. After all, the presence of a supernatural being can startle. Mary could have faced possible fear that Joseph would not believe her or the fear of public ridicule. However, I believe the angel was telling her not to fear or doubt the impossible. God can perform what seems impossible. He does not need your help. Your help leans on your own reasoning. This leads to fear. He does not need your fear. He needs your faith to birth blessings out of you.

Mary surrendered to the will of God. She realized that His plan was better than her plan. Therefore, she put her trust in

Reality Check

Him. Mary became a woman of faith. In Luke 1:46–55, Mary began magnifying the Lord, rejoicing in His greatness. She gave all glory and praise to God for honoring her humility with this blessing. After you have had a divine encounter with God, start rejoicing and give glory to His name. Declare His goodness with a joyful heart. Whatever He has promised will be manifested.

God blessed Mary without help from other people. Your dependence on others to bless you is conditional and limited. There are no limits with God. When you surrender to His will, as Mary did, He will utilize you as His vessel. You become a means through which His anointing will flow. You then become a blessing to others like Mary.

The angel informed Mary that her barren cousin Elisabeth was pregnant in her old age. Elisabeth was the one who was "called" barren. She was labeled as the one not able to birth new life. Have you been labeled negatively by others? Have you been told that you would not make it, you could not rise above your circumstances, or that your dreams could never become reality? This is what Elisabeth faced.

Although Elisabeth was called barren, the angel told Mary that Elisabeth was already six months pregnant. What a supernatural miracle! She only had three months remaining.

My sister, you may be pregnant with a blessing that you are unaware of at this time. While others are criticizing and labeling you, God can impregnate you with a miracle. Be encouraged! You could be more than halfway through to victory. You may only have a little while left. Now is not the time to give up. Let your faith arise!

Let us see how Elisabeth rejoices with Mary:

> And it came to pass, that when Elisabeth heard the salutation of Mary, the babe leaped in her womb; and Elisabeth was filled with the Holy Ghost: And she spake out with a loud voice, and said, Blessed art thou among women,

> and blessed is the fruit of thy womb. And whence is this to me, that the mother of my Lord should come to me? For, lo, as soon as the voice of thy salutation sounded in mine ears, the babe leaped in my womb for joy.
> —Luke 1:41–44, kjv

When Elisabeth heard Mary's greeting, she felt her baby leap. She could feel something stirring up within. It did not matter how she was formerly known. She knew that she was going to birth out a heaven-sent miracle. Like Elisabeth, you can also. God began working within you back when you felt like nothing was going on. In your darkest hours of life the conception of your miracle began taking place. You see, God births miracles out of famines, disasters, and heartbreaks. Get ready! Your miracle is about to leap.

God used Mary in such a powerful way, through revelation of His magnificent power. She gave birth to our Lord and Savior, Jesus Christ, who has redeemed us from the curse of sin. Elisabeth gave birth to John the Baptist who was anointed to preach repentance and prepared the way for the ministry of Jesus Christ. These two women were willing to live by God's divine plan. Are you willing?

Right now, begin to give Him thanks for who is He is and for His awesome power. Thank Him for the miracle that He has impregnated you with. Say this prayer:

> *Father, I come before You with honor, praise, and glory to Your Name. You have redeemed me from the curse of sin and its offspring through Jesus Christ Your Son. I thank You for making me a righteous and holy woman. I realize that I can do nothing without You. Therefore, I completely rely on, trust in, and depend on You. Although there have been times when I have felt totally alone and without hope, I realize now that You have never left my side. It was in those times that You brought conception to my miracle.*

Reality Check

Lord, I thank You for the blessing with which You have impregnated me. I know that the blessing being formed in my spiritual womb is leaping for joy. I thank You in advance for the manifestation of my miracle in accordance with Your divine purpose for my life. Amen.

CHAPTER 2

The Don'ts (Deception of Not Knowing God's Truths About Singleness) in a Relationship

YOU HAVE EXPLORED the reality check of how God's almighty power can be manifested as you submit to His divine will. Now you must move on to obeying His will in regards to your relationships with men. This seems to be a very difficult area for single women to yield over to God. Relationships for women have very strong emotional attachment. Because women are emotional creatures their feelings many times dominate their motives and actions. As a result, women can more easily surrender everything else in their lives over to God. However, women struggle giving up this area.

Ladies, you must understand that Satan is very familiar with your weaknesses in this arena. Therefore, this is where he will attack the strongest. God began dealing with me on this subject as I looked at my own life in retrospect. It became crystal clear to me that my focus had been off course. During those times, I longed for the presence of male companionship instead of the presence of God. I was twisted into a whirlwind of needless pains and sorrows. I thought that I needed to be with someone to feel loved, needed, and wanted. I searched for what I could never find outside of God.

I was deceived by Satan into entering this vicious cycle. I went from relationship to relationship. I struggled from one heartbreak to another. I would wonder what went wrong in search of something better. Satan in turn used those past hurts to elicit within me a low self-esteem, insecurity, and depression. He ultimately attempted to destroy God's divine plan for my future. Paul states in 2 Corinthians 2:11 (KJV), "Lest Satan should get an advantage of us; for we are not ignorant of his devices." Women, you must no longer be deceived. You must understand yourself, your actions, and most of all Satan's deceptive schemes in your relationships with men. Therefore ladies, please accompany me through a walk to discover the **D**eception **O**f **N**ot Knowing God's **T**ruths About **S**ingleness (DON'TS) in a relationship.

1. DON'T manipulate

First of all, I must establish my definition of manipulation. It is any form of maneuvering, altering, twisting, rearranging, or scheming with people, things, or circumstances to get what you want. Many women use this as means in their dealings with men. However, ladies, you must be aware of the seriousness of practicing manipulation. It can correspond with craftiness or sorcery. Witchcraft is a magical or irresistible influence, attraction, charm, or fascination. Galatians 5:19–21 (KJV) warns you against the use of witchcraft, "Now the works of the flesh are manifest, which are these; Adultery, fornication, uncleanness, lasciviousness, idolatry, witchcraft...that they which do such things shall not inherit the kingdom of God."

How do women manipulate men in relationships? There are internal and external sources of manipulation. An internal source is what you know to be called "mind games." Mind games involve strategically planting thoughts into his head or attempting to alter his thoughts in order to elicit a certain behavior. Another internal source involves appealing to his

The Don'ts in a Relationship

emotions and self-esteem such as provoking jealousy, using his weaknesses against him, threatening to reveal secrets, or challenging his manhood.

External sources of manipulation can include provocative behavior and seduction. As you just read in Galatians 5, fornication (sex outside of the marriage covenant) is also a work of the flesh and will exclude you from God's inheritance. Another external source is manipulating the people closest to him such as family or friends to get what you want.

Let us look at a biblical story of how a woman's influence altered her man's behavior through manipulation devised by Satan in the Garden of Eden:

> Now the serpent was more subtle and crafty than any living creature of the field which the LORD God had made. And he [Satan] said to the woman, Can it really be that God has said, You shall not eat from every tree of the garden? And the woman said to the serpent, We may eat the fruit from the trees of the garden, except the fruit from the tree which is in the middle of the garden. God has said, You shall not eat of it, neither shall you touch it, lest you die. But then the serpent said to the woman, You shall not surely die, For God knows that in the day you eat of it your eyes will be opened, and you will be like God, knowing the difference between good and evil and blessing and calamity. And when the woman saw that the tree was good (suitable, pleasant) for food and that it was delightful to look at, and a tree to be desired in order to make one wise, she took of its fruit and ate; and she gave some also to her husband and he ate.
> —GENESIS 3:1–6, AMP

Eve was manipulated and deceived by Satan's lies. She in turn somehow convinced Adam to eat of the fruit also. Could it be that Eve possibly had manipulated Adam, as Satan had manipulated her, to get what she wanted? Eve lusted for things that were outside of God's will for herself and her man. When you manipulate men in relationships, are you seeking God's will or earthly lust? Earthly lust is not limited to sexual lust. It is a carnal desire outside of the Spirit of God. We are told in Romans 8:5–6, "For they that are after the flesh do mind the things of the flesh; but they that are after the Spirit the things of the Spirit. For to be carnally minded is death; but to be spiritually minded is life and peace" (KJV).

Eve was warned that if she disobeyed His word, she would surely die. In other words, disobedience would cause physical and spiritual death. Eve separated herself from God, resulting in new trials, pains, and sorrows that previously did not exist. Their disobedience changed the course of their lives, bringing sin into the world. Animal sacrifices became required for the forgiving of sins. This was the Old Covenant law. Their disobedience ultimately gave Satan power as the prince of darkness of this world. However, because God is so merciful and loving, He redeemed you from this curse through Jesus Christ. This was the New Covenant.

Can you now see how manipulation has lasting effects? If you feel that you have to manipulate a man to keep him, then he may not be part of God's plan for your life in the first place. If you are dating someone that you are constantly manipulating, ask God to reveal to you His will regarding this relationship. If you are not dating anyone, ask God for preparation in avoiding the pitfalls of the enemy's deception through manipulation.

2. DON'T lose your self-respect

God created all women to be unique. Each one of you is valued highly as a priceless treasure to God. Unfortunately, many women do not see themselves the way God sees them. Failure to see your reflection in His eyes detours you to looking into the eyes of someone else in order to respect yourself. Satan traps women in this area. He orchestrates a cycle for women to behave in all acts of desperation. This in turn causes her to lose

The Don'ts in a Relationship

more self-respect and yield to more acts of desperation. Acts of desperation are things you do that you normally would not if you were in your "right" mind.

You can lose your self-respect through many avenues: insecurities, neediness, low self-esteem, depression, poor self-control, overreacting, and excessive compromising. Insecurities are usually birthed out of past hurts. You may have been lied to or abandoned in past relationships. These experiences tend to carry past hurts into new relationships, causing distrust and uncertainty. Insecurities can steer you to act out unnecessary behaviors of suspicion that he is "up to something." Many women secretly follow their men around and search their belongings. They are eager to accuse men of things when they may be completely innocent. This behavior can strain any relationship. You must come to understand that your security is in God.

Excessive neediness from women causes men to become very uncomfortable. It produces enormous pressure and drains them emotionally. It is impossible for any man to take God's place and fill your emptiness. A man may provide temporary relief, but this void will soon resurface. Excessive neediness results from a lack of understanding of God's desire to supply every need in your life.

The areas of low self-esteem and depression tend to coincide. We must first explore what causes this low self-esteem. Poor self-concepts can begin as early as childhood. Many women have suffered physical, verbal, emotional, sexual, and mental abuse as children. Abuse leaves emotional scars. In addition, as adults, they may have endured multiple heartbreaks, yielding low self-esteem and depression. When you do not esteem yourself or see your own self-worth, you tend to look to men to do it for you.

This can be an emotional roller coaster. Now, your personal happiness depends, first of all, on if you are in a relationship, and second, how you are treated. So, if you are not with anyone, you think there must be something wrong with you. If he says one day that you are beautiful, you feel beautiful. Another day, if he says you are ugly, you feel ugly. Once again, this is part of Satan's deception to keep you broken and miserable.

No matter what pains you have experienced in your past, Jesus can heal you and give you peace. Isaiah 53:5 (KJV) states, "But he was wounded for our transgressions, he was bruised for our iniquities: the chastisement of our peace was upon him; and with his stripes we are healed." Christ will give you a new self-esteem from His point of view. Would you not rather believe what Christ says about you, as opposed to anyone else? Let us take a closer look at what Jesus said in the defense of a woman about to be stoned to death by a group of men:

> The scribes and the Pharisees brought a woman caught in adultery, and having set her in the center of the court, they said to Him, "Teacher, this woman has been caught in adultery, in the very act. Now the Law Moses commanded us to stone such women; what then do You say?" They were saying this, testing Him, so that they might have ground for accusing Him. But Jesus stooped down and with His finger wrote on the ground. But when they persisted in asking Him, He straightened up, and said to them, "He who is without sin among you, let him be the first to throw a stone at her." Again He stooped down and wrote on the ground. When they heard it, they began to go out one by one, beginning with the older ones, and He was left alone, and the woman, where she was, in the center of the court. Straightening up, Jesus said to her, "Woman, where are they? Did no one condemn you?" She said, "No one, Lord." And Jesus said, "I do not condemn you, either. Go. From now on sin no more."
>
> —JOHN 8:3–11

Jesus set this woman free from her past. Perhaps she sought an adulterous relationship with a man that catered to her self-

The Don'ts in a Relationship

esteem. She could have been abused and neglected in her past. The Scribes and Pharisees did not respect this woman. Instead, they made a public spectacle of her. They were not concerned about her past hurts or abuse. They did not value her life. They were ready to stone her. Jesus always steps in right in the nick of time. He forgave her, restored her, and then sent her on her way. He has the same plan for you, my sister. He will give you back your self-respect.

Poor self-control and overreacting are usually based on emotions. Women are more easily motivated by their emotions. As a result, their actions and reactions reflect this. One of the fruits of the Spirit mentioned in Galatians 5:23 is temperance (self-control or self-restraint). Self-control will prevent you from overreacting when various circumstances arise in your relationship. A loss of self-control can lead you down a road you never thought you would take. It leads you into the "I just can't help myself" mode. Oh, but you can help yourself, by yielding yourself over to God and allowing His precious fruit to develop in your life.

In any relationship there must be compromise. However, there are cases when some women may feel the need to over-compromise themselves for men to the point of losing their identity somewhere in the process. Excessive compromising can mean giving up hopes, dreams, and aspirations. God has a plan for your life. You must hold on to it no matter what. If you are in a relationship that is compromising God's will for your life, then you are missing out. Do not give up your future for something or someone that is not part of God's future for you. You must become the woman that God created you to become. Respect who you are in Christ.

3. DON'T change your personality or compromise your values

Each woman is created to be unique. Her personality reflects her uniqueness. Some women are introverted and timid. Others are extroverted, bold, and outspoken. Most women fall somewhere between the two extremes. Regardless of the differences, everyone has had certain values instilled in them by people and past experiences. Your personality and values shape your identity.

If you are constantly altering your personality in a relationship, you must determine if you are doing so for self-improvement or for his satisfaction. I am not suggesting that all women are perfect without areas that need improvement. I am targeting the areas of your core personality that are precious and unique, and should be valued by any man. God made you the special person that you are. If you attempt to change your God-given personality, you are actually destroying His work. Has anyone ever told you that you have changed completely (usually for the worse) while you were dating a particular person? Were you doing things that you said you would never do? If so, most likely your personality and values were being altered.

Many women like velvet fabric for its smooth, elegant, and radiant appearance. Velvet is a pleasing material to run your fingers across. However, if you run your fingers against the grain of the fabric, it creates a rougher surface. The color tones of the fabric will not be uniform. As a result, the velvet loses its radiance. If you try to change whom God made you, you will lose your radiance. The main change that you should focus on is developing the character of Christ. I guarantee you these changes are always positive and are in agreement with God's will for your life.

Your most important value should be your relationship with Jesus Christ. He will reveal to you the areas that need to be changed. He is best at showing you yourself. He does not persecute but brings conviction to your heart through love. God chastises those He loves. (See Hebrews 12:6.) His love for you is genuine. Paul reveals in 1 Corinthians 13 God's definition of love:

Love endures long and is patient and kind; love never is envious nor boils over with jealousy, is not boastful or vainglorious, does not display itself haughtily. It is not conceited (arrogant and inflated with pride); it is not rude (unmannerly) and does not act unbecomingly. Love (God's love in us) does not insist on its own rights or its own way, for it is not self-seeking; it is not touchy or fretful or resentful; it takes no account of the evil done to it [it pays no attention to a suffered wrong]. It does not rejoice in injustice and unrighteousness, but rejoices when right and truth prevail. Love bears up under anything and everything that comes, is ever ready to believe the best of every person, its hopes are fadeless under all circumstances, and it endures everything [without weakening]. Love never fails [never fades out or becomes obsolete or comes to an end].
—1 CORINTHIANS 13:4–8, AMP

Now, ask yourself if the man in your relationship is trying to change you out to love or selfish motives. Next, ask yourself if you are trying to change him out of love or selfish motives. Remember, God is no respecter of persons. (See Acts 10:34.)

4. DON'T lie

Have you ever been in a relationship where you saw it necessary to lie to, stretch the truth with, or mislead him? If so, what were your motives? Did you really accomplish your mission? How did you feel as a result? Did you have peace or guilt? God feels so strongly against lying that he made it a commandment not to lie. (See Exodus 20:16.) You must understand that Satan is a liar and you are not to conform your ways to the character of the devil. Jesus said in John 8:44, "Ye are of your father the devil, and the lusts of your father ye will do. He was a murderer from the beginning, and abode not in the truth, because there is no truth in him. When he speaketh a lie, he speaketh of his own: for he is a liar, and the father of it" (KJV).

On the other hand, if God is your Father, your actions will reflect His character of truth and righteousness. Paul says in Ephesians 4:21–25, "If so be that ye have heard him, and have been taught by him, as the truth is in Jesus: That ye put off concerning the former conversation the old man, which is corrupt according to the deceitful lusts; And be renewed in the spirit of your mind; And that ye put on the new man, which after God is created in righteousness and true holiness. Wherefore putting away lying, speak every man truth with his neighbour: for we are members of one another" (KJV).

Maybe you have lied in your relationship only because you wanted to avoid penalty, confrontation, or disturbance. Or perhaps you just wanted to be right, look good, impress him, or obtain love and acceptance from him. Regardless of the reasons why you lied, they are still unacceptable in the eyes of your heavenly Father. God hates lies because He is all truth. The Bible says the truth sets us free and brings full liberty. (See John 8:32.) Do not let Satan's deception bring you under the bondage of lies.

Now that you know several reasons why women lie, we will explore some of the things that women lie about. Women have lied about their successes, failures, and intentions. They have lied regarding their mistakes, their past, other men, and even their whereabouts. Evaluate if the end result of your lies really achieved a real purpose. Think about the short-term and long-term effects. Lying in a relationship yields damaging effects that can ultimately destroy it. Rebekah orchestrated a deceptive plan. She had one of her sons lie to her husband pretending to be her other son in order to steal the blessing that did not belong to him. Let us read:

> Now it came about, when Isaac was old and his eyes were too dim to see, that he called his older son Esau and said to him, "My son." And he said to him, "Here I am." Isaac said, "Behold now, I am old and I do not know the day of my death. Now then, please take your gear, your quiver

The Don'ts in a Relationship

and your bow, and go out to the field and hunt game for me; and prepare a savory dish for me such as I love, and bring it to me that I may eat, so that my soul may bless you before I die." Rebekah was listening while Isaac spoke to his son Esau. So when Esau went to the field to hunt for game to bring home, Rebekah said to her son Jacob, "Behold I heard your father speak to your brother Esau, saying,...Now therefore, my son, listen to me as I command you. Go now to the flock and bring me two choice young goats from there, that I may prepare them as a savory dish for your father, such as he loves. Then you shall bring it to your father, that he may eat, so that he may bless you before his death."

—Genesis 27:1–7

With the help of Rebekah, Jacob lied to his father and received the blessing that belonged to his brother. Rebekah's deceptive scheme completely destroyed the two brothers' relationship and separated the family forever. Esau hated his brother Jacob so much that he planned to kill him. When Rebekah heard about this, she helped Jacob flee. Rebekah probably did not consider the lasting effects of lying. She could have thought she was doing this for the good of her son Jacob, and that God would understand.

Once again, lies are unacceptable in God's sight. However, because God was so merciful, He brought good out of this evil later in this story. Lying, like any sin, separates you from your Creator. In addition, it bruises and destroys relationships. If you are in God's will with your relationship, do not fall out of it into lies orchestrated by Satan to destroy your relationship. Accept God's truth and walk in liberty!

5. DON'T over-analyze

Too often, in relationships women over-analyze. They analyze everything men say, what they do, how they act, where they go, and whom they are with. I define over-analyzing as over-thinking or reprocessing your thoughts over and over again concerning circumstances that you alone cannot change. Satan frequently attacks this area of your mind through your thought processes. He heavily relies on penetrating your thought life through his deceptive schemes.

Over-processing your thoughts leads to unnecessary worry and stress that God does not intend for you to have. You are to cast all of our cares, anxieties, and worries on Christ. (See 1 Peter 5:7.) Romans 12:2 states, "And be not conformed to this world: but be transferred by the renewing of your mind, that ye may prove what is that good, and acceptable, and perfect, will of God" (KJV). Being conformed to this world involves being over-occupied with the cares of this world. If your mind is so preoccupied with everything going on around you, you will have difficulty discerning God's will for life.

Over-analyzing not only brings worry, but also fear. Most of the time this is fear of things that do not even exist. This fear creates stress, which is excessive strain on the mind or body. There are mental and physical manifestations of stress. Mental indicators of stress include increased annoyance or irritability, decreased motivation and creativity, and the inability to process your thoughts effectively.

Physical indicators of stress can include changes in your physical appearance, decreased sleep, changes in eating habits, and illness. This stress ultimately leads to complete exhaustion of your mental and physical strength, and collapse. Many women have exhausted all of their strength worrying over their relationship. They then rely on men for strength. They think they can no longer function without men.

This is Satan's deception. He does not want women to gain the knowledge of God's truth of where their strength really lies. Your strength comes from God your Father. Psalm 73:26 states, "My flesh and my heart may fail, but God is the Rock and firm Strength of my heart and my Portion forever" (AMP). He is the Rock on which you can build your foundation that

The Don'ts in a Relationship

will never fail. Let us review Christ's teaching on the two foundations:

> Therefore everyone who hears these words of Mine and acts on them, may be compared to a wise man who built his house on the rock. And the rain fell, and floods came, and the winds blew and slammed against that house; and yet it did not fall, for it had been founded on the rock. Everyone who hears these words of Mine and does not act on them, will be like a foolish man who built his house on the sand. The rain fell, and the floods came, and the winds blew and slammed against that house; and it fell—and great was its fall.
> —MATTHEW 7:24–27

Sister, if you rely on a man as your only foundation of strength, he will fail you greatly. Neither should you build your foundation on over-analyzing your thoughts and worrying. I assure you this is not God's plan for your life. Focus your mind on goodness, righteousness, and truth, as you surrender your thoughts to Him. As you communicate with God in prayer, He will free your mind with peace beyond your own understanding. (See Philippians 4:6–8.)

6. DON'T overwork

Society has taught women that they must apply strong effort and hard work in order to achieve success. This idea has in many cases been misinterpreted that if hard work is good, than overwork is better. Buying into this misconception in turn leads to the conclusion that you are valued only by the output of your overwork and not your input. Your outputs in a relationship are the things that you give out to him. This is your time, support, generosity, and commitment.

Your inputs in a relationship are the things that you "bring to the table" from the beginning. This is your personality, ideas, wit, interests, passions, values, and ingenuity. There must be a balance between inputs and outputs in any healthy relationship. Satan targets this area to bring imbalance causing you to overwork in the relationship to maintain equilibrium.

The inputs that a woman brings into a relationship are priceless and should be cherished and appreciated by her man. If her inputs are taken for granted and unappreciated, she may over-exhaust her outputs. She may give him all of her time or buy him gifts hoping to be appreciated. She is now overworking to impress him, please him, or keep him. This overproduction causes excessive wear and tear, and collapse.

Christ does not expect you to overwork to receive His gift of salvation, love, or acceptance. He certainly does not expect you to overwork to receive someone else's love and acceptance. Paul writes in Ephesians 2:8–10, "For by grace you have been saved through faith; and that not of yourselves, it is the gift of God; not as a result of works, so that no one may boast. For we are His workmanship, created in Christ Jesus for good works, which God prepared beforehand so that we would walk in them." You were predestined to do His good work. This involves expressing His love through your actions toward others so that He receives glory. God's divine plan involves "good work" not "overwork."

7. DON'T be overbearing

Do you remember an encounter with an overbearing schoolmate during your childhood or adolescence? Perhaps it was a young boy with a crush on you or a girl that wanted you for her best friend. Regardless who it was and the circumstances involved, you probably avoided this person. Most likely, this person's action was not meant to be overbearing, but simply to gain your attention or interest. However, the more overbearing this person became, the more likely you were to withdraw from him/her. As simple as this may seem, the same principle applies in adult relationships.

If you are in a relationship where you are too pushy with him, too controlling towards him, or just annoying him, then

The Don'ts in a Relationship

you are probably overbearing in this relationship. I am sure that you certainly do not mean any harm. However, operating in this exaggerated mode can leave him with a bad aftertaste. God does not instruct you to be overwhelming or domineering. He does instruct you to bear one another's burdens in order to lift each other up spiritually. (See Galatians 6:2.) Paul states in Romans 15:1–2: "Now we who are strong ought to bear the weaknesses of those without strength and not just please ourselves. Each of us is to please his neighbor for his good, to his edification." Is your overbearing behavior building him up spiritually or exhausting him mentally?

Women, you must be very careful not to confuse endurance with being overbearing. Most relationships will face trying times when it seems only endurance can hold things together. Endurance is that strength to stand firm under turmoil for an undetermined amount of time. Endurance builds character in your relationship. On the contrary, being overbearing can destroy your relationship. Do not allow Satan to mislead you down the road of falling into his deception from one broken relationship to another.

8. DON'T neglect your family and friends

Relationships can be very time-consuming. Any healthy relationship requires quality time in order for it to develop strong roots and blossom. However, many women have a misconception that a relationship must consume all their time. Therefore, they neglect time with family and friends. Satan will attempt to deceive you into thinking that if you do not spend all of your time with your man, you will lose him to someone else. Actually, a healthy relationship involves both parties keeping strong ties with others they care about. Have you ever been in a relationship where you felt pressure forcing you to choose between your family and friends, or him?

If so, did this pressure arise from him, your family, or yourself? This type of situation is very unpleasant and quite stressful. This pressure can be avoided by keeping your time balanced in order to fellowship with your family and friends, including the family of believers. Fellowship time has been emphasized throughout the New Testament among the body of Christ.

> We proclaim to you what we have seen and heard, so that you also may have fellowship with us. And our fellowship is with the Father and with his Son, Jesus Christ. We write this to make our joy complete. This is the message we have heard from him and declare to you: God is light; in him there is no darkness at all. If we claim to have fellowship with him yet walk in the darkness, we lie and do not live by the truth. But if we walk in the light, as he is in the light, we have fellowship with one another, and the blood of Jesus, his Son, purifies us from all sin.
>
> —1 JOHN 1:3–7, NIV

Women, always keep time available for fellowship with your friends, relatives, and your godly family. Your friends and family provide support and encouragement that cannot be substituted. The body of believers provides spiritual support and comfort. Your fellowship and support of one another demonstrates your fellowship with Christ.

> [I thank my God] for your fellowship (your sympathetic cooperation and contributions and partnership) in advancing the good news (the Gospel) from the first day [you heard it] until now. And I am convinced and sure of this very thing, that He Who began a good work in you will continue until the day of Jesus Christ [right up to the time of His return], developing [that good work] and perfecting and bringing it to full completion in you.
>
> —PHILIPPIANS 1:5–6, AMP

The Don'ts in a Relationship

Fellowship involves contributing quality time to others. In doing so, this enables Christ to perfect you according to His will for your life.

9. DON'T do things that you may regret later

Many times women have been pressured in relationships to go way out of their way making sacrifices that they really do not want to make. You can somehow find yourself vulnerable and going that extra mile for him only to find yourself regretful later. Relationships certainly involve give and take, but I am referring to the case where you are the only one giving in the relationship and he is the only one taking. Your kindness should not be misused or devalued.

You were created with unique gifts. Paul tells us in 1 Corinthians 7:7, "....But each has his own special gift from God, one of this kind and one of another" (AMP). He was referring to relationships with respect to deciding to marry versus remaining single. In other words, certain gifts enable some people to remain alone and other people to have a mate. Your gifts consist of certain qualities, talents, and abilities that enable you to give freely to others and bless them. First Peter 4:10 states, "Each one should use whatever gift he has received to serve others, faithfully administering God's grace in its various forms" (NIV). Because these gifts were given to you by God, they generally come very natural for you.

In a relationship, it is far easier to operate within your gifts than outside of them. Gifts should demonstrate the love of Jesus Christ within you. A sense of regret and frustration can result from attempting to function in other gifts that do not belong to you. Therefore, use your gifts wisely and generously within your relationship. However, do not continue doing things that your gifts have not enabled you to do.

10. DON'T look to him as your primary source of fulfillment

Many women are not fulfilled in their relationships because

they are looking to men as their primary source of fulfillment instead of God. A life of fulfillment can only come from drawing your source from your Almighty Father. Do you remember any dry summer day when nothing could quench your thirst like cool water? As you drank the water, do you remember feeling the gentle flow of complete satisfaction transfuse your body? This spiritual type of thirst is described in Psalm 42:1–2, "As the deer pants for streams of water, so my soul pants for you, O God. My soul thirst for God, for the living God. When can I go and meet with God?" (NIV).

This same thirst has driven many women from relationship to relationship, yearning for God's living water just like the Samaritan woman at the well. Let us read:

> There came a woman of Samaria to draw water. Jesus said to her, "Give Me a drink." For His disciples had gone away into the city to buy food. Therefore, the Samaritan woman said to Him, "How is it that You, being a Jew, ask me for a drink since I am a Samaritan woman?" (For Jews have no dealings with Samaritans.) Jesus answered and said to her, "If you knew the gift of God, and who it is who says to you, 'Give Me a drink,' you would have asked Him, and He would have given you living water." She said to Him, "Sir, You have nothing to draw with and the well is deep; where then do You get that living water? You are not greater than our father Jacob, are You, who gave us the well, and drank of it himself and his sons and his cattle?" Jesus answered and said to her, "Everyone who drinks of this water will thirst again; but whoever drinks of the water that I will give him shall never thirst; but the water that I will give him will become in him a well of water springing up to eternal life." The woman said to Him, "Sir, give me this water, so I will not be thirsty nor come all the way here to draw."
>
> —JOHN 4:7–15

The Don'ts in a Relationship

This powerful passage demonstrates God's ability to reveal Himself as a woman's true source. This woman had a desperate thirst for what the men in her life were unable to quench. She knew about God, but she did not know him as her source of joy, peace, and contentment. Many Christian women find themselves in the same predicament even though they go to church, sometimes read the Bible and pray, and may be involved in a ministry. You must develop a personal relationship with Christ in order to draw from His well.

The Samaritan woman questioned how Jesus could draw water from a well that was so deep. Have you ever questioned if Jesus could really reach those broken areas so deep within you? I encourage you that He certainly can! Jesus is waiting to converse with you just as He did with the Samaritan woman. The problem that many women have when approaching Him is that they are hesitant to lay the whole truth out before Him.

When Jesus told the Samaritan woman to bring her husband to Him, she told Him the truth. Then, He began revealing information to her about her life. (See John 4:16–18.) Jesus already knew about her past mistakes and present circumstances before He asked her, but He needed for her to trust Him enough to tell Him the truth about herself. Women, do not try to cover up your mistakes when you are before His presence. Openly lay your life before Him. He will create a well deep within you, springing up His living water. This will finally quench your thirst. Look to God as your source of fulfillment, and you will never thirst again.

CHAPTER 3

As She Waits

GOD'S DIVINE PLAN for your life will involve overcoming past relationships and waiting in His presence for your future mate. You have a choice to either wait on God for the man He created you for, or choose your own husband without Him. God knows you better than you know yourself. God knew about you before you were ever born. God told Jeremiah, "Before I formed you in the womb, I knew you" (Jer. 1:5). Because He created you, He knows the blueprint of your spiritual, physical, emotional, and mental makeup. Therefore, if there is a malfunction in any of these areas, He sees exactly where the breakdown has occurred. He is a more than qualified mechanic to fix it. He knows every soft, smooth, hard, and jagged edge that forms you.

He also knows all the same areas of your future husband. God has already done a background check on the husband that He has given you before he was born. God forms the "perfect fit" when he unites you with your husband. He said that when a man and woman marry, they become one flesh. (See Genesis 2:24.) It is much simpler for two people, whose union God predestined, to blend together as one flesh than two people that He has not predestined. Are you a woman willing to wait in His presence for your husband? Or will you rely on your own thoughts and insight? Only you can decide.

Many single Christian women say that they are waiting on God for their husbands because it makes them feel good and makes others think well of them. However, the truth is, it is very convenient to make this claim when you are not dating anybody at the time. However, as soon as you meet somebody you want to date, you totally forget about God's divine will. I call this the "I'm waiting on God for my husband" cliché.

Sadly enough, waiting for God has become a simple cliché that is used when convenient and it feels good. Imagine how God feels as He is waiting to bless His daughters with the husbands blueprinted for them. However, instead of waiting in His presence, they are dating other men outside of His will while telling others that they are waiting on Him. This would greatly disappoint any father. Do not fall into the "I'm waiting on God for my husband" cliché. Instead, really mean it when you say it.

Women fear waiting on God because they think it will take longer than they are willing to wait. God does not make you wait to drag things out and exhaust you. On the contrary, as you wait, He strengthens you. We are told in Psalm 27:14, "Wait on the LORD: be of good courage, and he shall strengthen thine heart: wait, I say, on the LORD" (KJV). Let this time be a period of spiritual growth and development as He prepares you for your future.

Jesus revealed to me a modern-day illustration of myself waiting in His presence. Jesus and I were walking together in a large crowded shopping mall. We arrived at a food court area where we sat and conversed about His plans for my future. After this, He told me He was leaving and would return, and I needed to stay seated there and wait for him. In the beginning, the wait was not so bad because I had just been with Jesus and I figured He would return fairly quickly. However, as time passed, I had to put my faith to work and trust that He had not

As She Waits

forgotten me. I had to believe what He told me and remain obedient to His instructions.

While I was sitting alone at the food court, I began to see some familiar faces. They came by and asked me why was I sitting there alone. I told them I was waiting for Jesus. They asked me how long was I going to wait. I responded that I would wait for Him until He returned. They seemed very puzzled by my response and suggested that I check out of some the attractions at the mall, but I declined. The mall was full of people with shopping bags who seemed discontent, in search of something they could not find.

As I waited, His perfect peace engulfed me even though I was surrounded by mass confusion. There were numerous distractions available to deter my focus. I avoided them and kept my mind on Him. I had many opportunities to get anxious, afraid, and angry, because He had not returned by the time that I thought He should have. It did not feel good sitting there. My emotions told me I must have only dreamt about this encounter with Him or He must have forgotten me and I should just give up. Yet, I waited with a positive attitude. I remembered His words, and I trusted that He would return just as He said. Although time grew short and the picture appeared grim, I began to sing praises to His name and worship Him just for who He was.

As I worshiped Him, His glory fell upon me and I could see myself the way He saw me. His plans for my future became crystal clear. My faith had elevated to a new level as I waited for what seemed impossible. Patience was doing its perfect work within me. He was perfecting me with sweet peace and gentle patience. These two form a powerful combination. As I replaced my waiting on Him with just worshiping Him, He suddenly reappeared again. This is because He dwells in the midst of worship. You see, I thought I was waiting on Jesus. He was actually waiting on me. He was already present. It was my worship that revealed His presence to me.

Women, each of you has a choice. You can remain still and transform your waiting to worship, or you can grow impatient and allow distractions to take you out of His presence. What will you choose? Remember, the next time you say, "I'm waiting on God for my husband" your actions will speak much louder than your words.

WWW.keyword

Women, you are bombarded with enormous amounts of information via the world-wide-web. You simply type in "www." plus the keyword of our interest and you obtain unlimited information. This same process also can be applied when waiting on God for an answer or a miracle. I call it the WWW. keyword or "**W**orship **W**hile you **W**ait.**keyword**" process of waiting for your miracle.

You must apply the correct spiritual keys to yield God's unlimited promises. God has a prosperous future planned for every area of your life. God told His people in Jeremiah 29:11–13, "'For I know the plans I have for you,' declares the LORD, 'plans to prosper you and not to harm you, plans to give you hope and future. Then you will call upon me and come and pray to me, and I will listen to you. You will seek me and find me when you seek me with all your heart'" (NIV).

You must seek God with all of your heart, through intimate worship, which begins with developing a personal relationship with Jesus Christ. It is very difficult if not impossible to wait, rely, or trust in someone that you do not know. Therefore, you cannot wait in God's presence if you do not know Him.

With this in mind, we will examine ten "keywords" or principles in order to worship while you wait.

1. WWW.find yourself in Christ

You must first accept Jesus Christ as your Lord and Savior to receive the gift of eternal life. Jesus tells us in John 14:6, "I am the way, and the truth, and the life; no one comes to the Father

As She Waits

but through Me." You can only find your new life through Jesus Christ by giving up your former life. Jesus says in Matthew 16:25, "For whosoever will save his life shall lose it: and whosoever will lose his life for my sake shall find it" (KJV). Many people share the misconception that their good works will attain them high status with God. On the contrary, you are saved by the loving grace of God and not by any of your good works, successes, or achievements. Therefore, no one can brag or boast that they are better than someone else. (See Ephesians 2:8–9.)

Your new identity in Christ will yield His character in every aspect of your life. People will notice this change in you almost immediately. You will certainly notice this change within yourself. It will affect how you think, how you react, where you go, and what you say. The most outstanding characteristic of Christ is His overpowering love.

As you find yourself in Him, you will share in this love as you interact with others. You will have a greater affection for people. You will overlook people's faults and forgive them more easily. You will also demonstrate patience and a greater tolerance for others. You will have stronger compassion for them. This is what Paul describes in Ephesians 4:2, "Be completely humble and gentle; be patient, bearing with one another in love" (NIV). You see, finding yourself in Christ ultimately affects everyone around you.

2. WWW.discover Christ's purpose for your life

God desires to give you a vision of your divine destiny so that you will not live in hopelessness. As described in Proverbs 29:18, "Where there is no vision, the people perish" (KJV). People lose hope in their purpose for living without a vision of how God sees them. A vision is a revelation from God Himself showing you how you fit into the scheme of things in His divine plan. God is in the business of performing big miracles beyond what you can imagine in your own mind. He deposits a vision within your spirit far beyond what your mind could ever create.

Once you receive a vision of His purpose for your life, you must believe it. As Paul described in Ephesians 3:20, "Now unto him that is able to do exceedingly abundantly above all that we ask or think, according to the power that worketh in us" (KJV). You play an important role in whether or not your vision will become a reality. You will have to live by faith.

Many times women have depended on the faith of their parents, grandparents, pastors, or other church leaders. This time has passed. Women, it is time to step up to the plate and face it head on. I assure you it is well worth it. If your vision seems too great to be real, believe it and thank God for it anyway. If you do, it will surely come to pass just as He told you.

3. WWW.pray

Prayer is the most powerful tool you have in accessing His divine will. Sadly, many Christians do not use this tool. Prayer enables open communication with your Divine Maker. We are told in 1 Thessalonians 5:17, "Pray without ceasing" (KJV), and in Ephesians 6:18, "Praying always with all prayer and supplication in the Spirit." (KJV). If prayer was not important, God would not have told you to do it. Some people have a misconception that prayer is useless because they do not see any action going on while they are praying. To the contrary, prayer can directly link you into destroying strongholds in your life and yield unlimited blessings.

Prayer is not just your pastor's responsibility—it is also yours. Stop depending on others to access God for you. He is waiting right now for you to come before Him where His grace is so rich, as described in Hebrews 4:16, "Let us therefore come boldly unto the throne of grace, that we may obtain mercy, and find grace to help in time of need" (KJV). Prayer is your only real help during the time of need.

Do not make prayer a rare and unfamiliar part of your life. Pray daily. Jesus Christ has made you His personal friend. (See John 15:14). He has told you in His word to pray. Do you com-

As She Waits

municate regularly with your closest friends? If Christ is your friend, you will communicate with Him daily and your friendship will grow deeper and deeper.

4. WWW.study the Word

There is no other book more valuable for your spiritual walk with God than the Holy Bible. It contains God's spoken words or truths in action. Second Timothy 2:15 states, "Study to show thyself approved unto God, a workman that needeth not to be ashamed, rightly dividing the word of truth" (KJV). The only way to know God's truth is to read His word. The Bible reveals real life stories of people's trials and triumphs as they endured to the end. God used the lives of these people to be a testimony to you today. His word unlocks mysteries from how this world was created to how it will end.

The Bible gives specific instructions on how to live a Godly lifestyle. It points out the keys to obtaining success in your daily living. In addition, the Bible contains direct teachings of Jesus Christ when He was on earth and of the Holy Spirit after His ascension. Studying the Word of God familiarizes you with your heritage and reveals your future inheritance in Him. You will better understand your roots and learn powerful testimonies by reading the Bible. In addition, through reading, studying, and meditating on His Word, you will discover the power of the blood of Jesus, and how to live through the guidance of the Holy Spirit.

5. WWW.look to Jesus as your source

We explored in the previous chapter how only Jesus Christ can be your source of living water to quench your thirst. Now you will progress to abiding in Him as your source of life as Christ stated:

> I am the true vine, and My Father is the vinedresser. Every branch in Me that does not bear fruit, He takes away; and every branch that bears fruit, He prunes it so

that it may bear more fruit. You are already clean because of the word which I have spoken to you. Abide in Me, and I in you. As the branch cannot bear fruit of itself unless it abides in the vine, so neither can you unless you abide in Me. I am the vine, you are the branches; he who abides in Me and I in him, he bears much fruit, for apart from Me you can do nothing. If anyone does not abide in Me, he is thrown away as a branch and dries up; and they gather them, and cast them in the fire and they are burned. If you abide in Me, and My words abide in you, ask whatever you wish and it will be done for you.
—JOHN 15:1–7

Do you ever feel empty and lifeless within your spirit? If so, you must abide in Jesus as your lifeline. You can only obtain the fruits of the Spirit as you stay connected with Him. (See Galatians 5:22—24.) Abiding in Him continually revitalizes you because His royal blood is now flowing through your veins. You must understand that without Christ you will become spiritually lifeless, although everything on the outside might appear normal. As you abide in Him, His will for your life will become more apparent to you. You will begin praying according to His will and He will grant it.

When Christ is your life source, people will look at you in amazement of how you can look so vibrant to keep so much joy. People would spend millions to obtain this life source that God gives freely to those who just simply want it. The value of abiding in Him is priceless. He will continue developing the fruits of love, joy, peace, gentleness, kindness, faith, and patience in your life only as you look to Him as your only life source. These fruits will become sweeter each day and give off a delightful flavor to all that taste of them.

6. WWW.hunger and thirst after righteousness

Because God is righteous, His presence in your life will cause you to seek after righteousness. Righteousness involves

As She Waits

being in right standing with God. This means having a godly lifestyle. It will reflect where you go, what you do, what you say, how you dress, and how you act. If you are truly hungering and thirsting for right standing with God, He will fill you to the point of satisfaction. Jesus states in Matthew 5:6, "Blessed are those who hunger and thirst for righteousness, for they shall be satisfied." Have you ever craved a particular food and nothing else could satisfy you until you finally ate it? In like manner, God puts a craving within you for His righteousness, which only He can fill.

Many people question if there are shady areas of living godly. An excellent way to assess questionable circumstances is to ask yourself if you could truly imagine Jesus Christ doing the same thing if He were in your position. Christ did not walk in shadiness or grayness, but in the light of righteousness and truth. Therefore, if you feel a spiritual uneasiness about something you are doing, it is better to stop it altogether. There are blessings in living righteous before God. So, guard all that you do with His righteous approval so that you may stand up right before Him.

7. WWW.keep a positive attitude

Your attitude will determine your magnitude of blessing. A joyful heart creates a positive attitude and a positive attitude creates a joyful heart. A positive attitude not only affects you, but every one that comes into contact with you. Can you recall being around a positive person? It just seems to make a calming and reassuring atmosphere. It certainly sends mixed messages to others when you say that you are a Christian, but have a bad attitude.

Your new life in Christ should change your attitude as Paul reminds us in Ephesians 4:22-24, "You were taught, with regard to your former way of life, to put off your old self, which is being corrupted by its deceitful desire; to be made new in the attitude of your minds; and to put on the new self, created to be like God in true righteousness and holiness" (NIV). It is beneficial for you to change your way of thinking to reflect positive thoughts, which will change your attitude. The choice is yours whether or not you will receive all that God has in store for you depending on your attitude.

Negative thoughts can lead to murmuring, complaining, and faultfinding. In this situation, you would not be able to discern God's will for your life, even if He stood right in front of you and told you. This would be because your mind would not be renewed. God is not pleased with people who bicker and complain. He cannot bless them. Remember how the Israelites wandered in the wilderness for forty years and never entered the Promised Land due to their lack of faith, bad attitudes, and persistent complaining? A negative attitude has long-lasting consequences. Keep in mind the magnitude of God's goodness, mercy, and loving-kindness towards you. Keep a positive attitude.

8. WWW.get busy doing God's work

As you worship God, your heart will begin to sense the heart of God. His desires will become your desires, such as witnessing to nonbelievers, getting more involved in your local church, and sharing your personal testimony. Do not fall into the "There are plenty of people doing God's work and He doesn't need me" mentality. Your position is just as important to Him as the next person. Actually, it is your responsibility to work for Him. Someone's life may depend on your cooperation.

There is much work that needs to be done for His kingdom. Jesus told His followers in Luke 10:2, "The harvest is plentiful, but the workers are few. Ask the Lord of the harvest, therefore, to send out workers into his harvest field" (NIV). Christ is just waiting for laborers who are willing to work for Him. When your focus is on pursuing the work of God, your personal needs will automatically be provided for. Jesus stated in Matthew 6:33, "But seek first His kingdom and His righteousness, and all these things will be added to you." These "things" are your personal needs such as food, clothing, shelter, money, and transportation, among others.

Doing God's work can enable Him to provide you with all that you need, thus freeing you from worry and anxiety. Paul tells us in 1 Corinthians 15:58, "Therefore, my dear brothers, stand firm. Let nothing move you. Always give yourselves fully to the work of the Lord, because you know that your labor in the Lord is not in vain" (NIV). Your work for God is not a waste of your time.

9. WWW.wait for God

It may seem redundant to the theme of this chapter of worshiping while you wait to reemphasize waiting for God. However, as Paul states in Ephesians 6:13, "And having done all, to stand" (KJV). I challenge you to do all you can to wait on God—just wait! Waiting is an active process in which you are standing by faith on God's Word for whatever you are hoping for. You cannot just sit around twiddling your thumbs and humming hopeless melodies, thinking somehow, by chance, your ship may come in someday. No, your faith will bring your ship into existence!

Understand this, whatever God has in store for you is worth waiting for. He is on your side. Isaiah 64:4 states, "For from days of old they have not heard or perceived by ear, nor has the eye seen a God besides You, who acts in behalf of the one who waits for Him." God will act on your behalf if you wait for Him to do so. You must yield to God's timing and not your own timing.

Impatience causes you to attempt to take circumstances into your own hands by acting prematurely. This always leads you to disappointment. God will not speed up His perfect timing due to your impatience. Actually, impatience has a large impact on delaying His timing for your miracle. Therefore, when God promises you something, He expects you to diligently wait for His intervention. So ladies, just wait!

10. WWW.serve others

Jesus Christ commanded you to love one another in the same way that He has loved you. (See John 15:12.) Serving others is an expression of God's love working through you. It involves giving, sacrificing, assisting, and caring for the needs of others without expecting anything in return. This is the heart of a servant of God. Christ Himself became a servant in order to deliver us from sin. As stated in Philippians 2:5–8, "Your attitude should be the same as that of Christ Jesus: who, being in very nature God, did not consider equality with God something to be grasped, but made himself nothing, taking the very nature of a servant, being made in human likeness. And being found in appearance as a man, he humbled himself and became obedient to death—even death on a cross!" (NIV).

Because Christ made such a sacrifice in becoming a servant for your sake, how much more should you be willing to serve others for His sake? Serving others not only gives them an opportunity to see God's love through you. It also allows God to see your love for Him. If you love Christ, you will obey his instructions. When God saved you, He rescued you from the bondage of sin and gave you freedom. Paul states in Galatians 5:13, "For you were called to freedom, brethren; only do not turn your freedom into an opportunity for the flesh, but through love serve one another." Do not allow the bondage of selfishness to stop you from being the servant God enabled you to be. Serve others and take your freedom.

WAITING WITH PATIENCE

Patience is the inner strength to maintain peace, rest, and flexibility as you wait for God's divine intervention. You have the ability to allow patience to flow in your life. James 1:4 states, "But let patience have her perfect work, that ye may be perfect and entire, wanting nothing" (KJV). You must allow patience

As She Waits

the opportunity to perfect the work of Christ within you. He perfects you through trials and furnaces of affliction over time so that you may grow up in Him and never lack.

Patience signifies growth and maturity. Do you remember as a child wanting something immediately from your parents with little or no ability to patiently wait for it? Because you were only a child, you lacked the wisdom and understanding of why you needed to wait for certain things from your parents. Similarly, as children of God, you can also lack wisdom and knowledge as to why you must wait on your heavenly Father. As you mature in Christ, you begin to gain wisdom and clear understanding of His ways thus yielding this inner strength known as patience.

Patience enables you to maintain your cool during the storms of life. Proverbs 24:10 states, "If you faint in the day of adversity, your strength is small" (AMP). If you give up or give out when times are tough, your patience is small or limited. Patience has the ability to carry you through a storm. You gain the knowledge power that Christ is with you during the storm, and He has a miracle waiting when the storm is over. Proverbs 24:5 states, "A wise man is strong, and a man of knowledge increases power." You gain power through your understanding of who Christ is in your life. Put your complete trust in Him and wait for Him.

Patience allows God's provision to work on your behalf. Impatience causes irritability and the inability to remain still. If you are constantly hurrying and trying to make things happen yourself, you are blocking God's provision in your life. You must be still through patience to see God's intervention within your situation. Patience enables you to stop asking God how long and start professing that you are holding on!

Waiting With Expectation

Your miracle is a physical manifestation to you of what God accomplished for you in the spiritual realm. Expecting your miracle is a spiritual manifestation of your faith in Him. Miracles do not come without expectation. When Christ performed numerous miracles of healings, recoveries of sight, and raisings from the dead, He expected the miracle to come forth by faith. You also must begin to expect the miracles that God has promised you.

Do not confuse expectation with pride. Expectation results from your faith in God. Pride results from your faith in yourself. Expectation boldly professes that there are no limits to God's miracles concerning you. You can do all that He gives you the ability to do. Paul states in Philippians 4:13, "I can do all things through Him who strengthens me." Through Christ, you can expect supernatural intervention on your behalf while you are waiting for it.

Expectation changes your way of thinking from self-assurance to God-assurance. You can be God-assured that He is working on your behalf. He is calling light out of the dark areas in your life. He is making crooked ways straight. He is creating new life all around you where there was once death. As you gain insight on God's unlimited resources, you gain greater understanding in what you can expect. You are told in Proverbs 24:14, "So shall you know skillful and godly Wisdom to be thus to your life; if you find it, then shall there be a future and a reward, and your hope and expectation shall not be cut off" (AMP). Your miracle and divine future awaits you! Expect great things from him and watch the promises unfold.

Waiting With Endurance

Endurance can be used interchangeably with perseverance, persistence, and continuance. Endurance is the ability to hold your ground and remain consistent despite temptation, discomfort, and other negative circumstances. A woman that endures may make mistakes and even fall multiple times, but she will get right back up and continue her course. Proverbs 24:16 states, "For a righteous man falls seven times, and rises again." Do not give up because you may have fallen or gotten off course, but get up in the name of Jesus and press on to your miracle.

The key to endurance is remaining grounded in Jesus Christ and staying anchored in His word. You must become determined to stay connected with godly people, keep going to church, and keep sin out of your life. Remember that these circumstances will not last forever. Change will come as you endure. If everything in life were delivered to you on a silver platter, you would not need to persevere and trust in God. Paul reminds you, "But if we hope for what we do not see, with perseverance we wait eagerly for it" (Rom. 8:25).

Too often, people want things handed to them with little effort involved. If you are going to endure for your divine destiny, you will need to bring a change of clothes. Roll up your sleeves, be ready to get your hands dirty, and get to work. Certainly your miracle is a free gift from God, but the journey to your miracle will require endurance.

Your ability to endure will depend on your trial threshold. This is the threshold level in which you are able bear certain trials before giving up or calling quits. People with low trial thresholds cannot endure much. They just throw in the towel and never reach their destination. On the other hand, those who develop high trial thresholds do not quickly give up. They realize that their circumstances may appear hopeless, but they endure anyway. These people press on to the end to receive their reward. Build a high trial threshold and hold on until the end. Remember, those that endure will receive the reward.

CHAPTER 4

From Pain to Purpose

As HUMAN BEINGS, we all have suffered emotional pain at some point in our lives. Too often, however, women have managed to hold on to painful experiences. They have allowed these experiences to shape their personalities, mold their character, control their actions, and shatter their futures. Pain can be all that many women can identify with. It merely becomes a way of life for them. Perhaps they have been so accustomed to pain that holding on to it provides comfort and protection from the unknown or unfamiliar.

Pain is hurtful, uncomfortable, and yields lasting effects. However, the good news is that these lasting effects do not have to be negative ones. Jesus already carried your pains and sorrows back when He died on the cross. Now it is just a matter of you laying down your pains on the cross. He will do the rest. Jesus rearranges the secret components of pain and transforms it into a miracle as a result.

The secret components of pain are the areas of pain that can directly affect your life. It may make no sense to you how a painful experience could penetrate through secret areas within your core being while you were unaware. Often, you are only made aware of its effects when it resurfaces through a new incident, relationship, or other circumstance. Many women feel defeated by past hurts and have difficulty escaping its powerful grip. Most of the time, the long-term deteriorating effects of pain far outweigh the actual experience that occurred in the past. You must come to understand these secret components of pain to better appreciate the work Jesus Christ will perform deep within these unreachable places.

Frequently, pain is thought to only have negative consequences, with the exception of pain resulting from physical exercise. It is well understood that while exercise may be uncomfortable, it is good for the body, creating the popular cliché "NO PAIN, NO GAIN." To your surprise, through God, you can also gain from your pain. You might ask, "How could this be?" Although you may have endured painful experiences that you cannot talk about, God has the power to create your divine destiny out of the secret components of past pain. He takes what Satan meant for evil and turns it into good because He loves you.

Through pain you gain a greater understanding of God's love for you. There is no pain too great for the Master's touch. Just one touch from Him can set you free. Your pain will not destroy you. To the contrary, it will reconstruct you into a woman of strength and purpose through Christ Jesus. He endured unimaginable pain on the cross with a purpose in mind. His purpose was to deliver you from the bondage of sin and transform you into a righteous and victorious woman. The pain that you have suffered has not been in vain. Christ will transform your pain into His divine purpose.

Why Pain?

You may often wonder why pain is necessary in life. After all, it certainly does not feel good. If you had a choice, would you choose a life with or without pain? The answer may seem obvious. However, the less likely choice is the best answer. For

From Pain to Purpose

women, pain entered this world as a result of sin. Remember in the Garden of Eden, when Eve ate of the forbidden fruit in disobedience to God? God told her that she would endure pain during the birthing process as a result:

> To the woman He said, "I will greatly multiply your pain in childbirth, in pain you will bring forth children."
> —Genesis 3:16

This was the beginning of pain for women. In addition, animal sacrifices had to be made to God after giving birth on the woman's behalf for purification:

> Then the Lord spoke to Moses, saying "Speak to the sons of Israel, saying: 'When a woman gives birth and bears a male child, then she shall be unclean for seven days, as in the days of her menstruation she shall be unclean. On the eighth day the flesh of his foreskin shall be circumcised. Then she shall remain in the blood of her purification for thirty-three days; she shall not touch any consecrated thing, nor enter the sanctuary until the days of her purification are completed. But if she bears a female child, then she shall be unclean to two weeks, as in her menstruation; and she shall remain in the blood of her purification for sixty-six days. When the days of her purification are completed, for a son or for a daughter, she shall bring to the priest at the doorway of the tent of meeting a one year old lamb for a burnt offering and a young pigeon or a turtledove for a sin offering. Then he shall offer it before the Lord and make atonement for her, and she shall be cleansed from the flow of her blood. This is the law for her who bears a child, whether a male or a female. But if she cannot afford a lamb, then she shall take two turtledoves or two young pigeons, the one for a burnt offering and the other for a sin offering; and the priest shall make atonement for her, and she will be clean.'"
> —Leviticus 12:1–8

By this point, women had to suffer the pain of giving birth, followed by making offerings to God in order to purify themselves. Purification follows pain. Although one woman sinned in the Garden of Eden, bringing pain upon all women, God had a plan for purification. God does nothing without purpose. The length of time for the purification process after giving birth to a male child versus a female child differed also. Perhaps this represented differences in the components of pain between women and men. Keep in mind, God makes no mistakes. Now we can begin to unfold the divine will of God as a result of pain after Mary gave birth to Christ:

> And when eight days were accomplished for the circumcising of the child, his name was called JESUS, which was so named of the angel before he was conceived in the womb. And when the days of her purification according to the law of Moses were accomplished, they brought him to Jerusalem, to present him to the Lord; (As it is written in the law of the Lord, Every male that openeth the womb shall be called holy to the Lord;) And to offer a sacrifice according to that which is said in the law of the Lord, a pair of turtledoves, or two young pigeons.
> —LUKE 2:21–24, KJV

We see here that Mary, the mother of Jesus, had to pass through the process of pain and purification for the purpose of giving birth to Jesus. Yet, it does not stop there. God took the pain that began with the sin of Eve, and brought forth His own Son, Jesus, into the world to bear the pain of the cross for the divine purpose of salvation, deliverance, and healing to every area if your life. He became the holy and living sacrifice for your purification.

Perhaps your past hurts may have left you bleeding, feeling dirty, hopeless, alone, and ashamed. Your emotions may be bleeding from abuse, neglect, rejection, or depression. Take courage my sister, and reach out to Him! One touch of Jesus

From Pain to Purpose

will completely purify you and stop your bleeding, just like the woman in this passage:

> A large crowd followed and pressed around him. And a woman was there who had been subject to bleeding for twelve years. She had suffered a great deal under the care of many doctors and had spent all she had, yet instead of getting better she grew worse. When she heard about Jesus, she came up behind him in the crowd and touched his cloak, because she thought, "If I just touch his clothes, I will be healed." Immediately her bleeding stopped and she felt in her body that she was freed from her suffering. At once Jesus realized that power had gone out from him. He turned around in the crowd and asked, "Who touched my clothes?" "You see the people crowding against you," his disciples answered, "and yet you can ask, 'Who touched me?'" But Jesus kept looking around to see who had done it. Then the woman, knowing what had happened to her, came and fell at his feet and, trembling with fear, told him the whole truth. He said to her, "Daughter, your faith has healed you. Go in peace and be freed from your suffering."
>
> —MARK 5:24–34, NIV

After touching Jesus she became purified, and the pain and bleeding subsided. This woman had a testimony with greater understanding of who Jesus really was. He moved her from bleeding pain into His divine purpose. She may have endured twelve years of pain, but suddenly her day of deliverance had arrived. Furthermore, Jesus will replenish you with more than the years, time, money, and relationships that you lost. Your greatest pain could be forming your greatest miracle right now. Your pain will be your gain.

REJECTION YIELDS CORRECTION

Rejection is a precursor to pain. Moreover, rejection is intensely painful when utilized by those you love and trust. If you have felt pain through rejection by someone that you did not care about, most likely your ego was insulted, resulting from pride. Insulting your pride penetrates the carnal mind, but rejection penetrates the heart. It is comforting to your heart to know that those you love and trust feel the same toward you. When these feelings are not mutual, rejection results.

Rejection lures you into a series of attempts to correct things in order to make this person accept you. You may overcompensate to obtain love and affection, but never accomplish your goal. Does this sound familiar? If so, realize that you deserve far better. You do not have to try to correct your rejection because Christ will do it for you. He is all too familiar with rejection. He was rejected by His own people and was put to death on the cross by them. But through this rejection He yielded correction when He rose again and now sits on the throne at the right hand of God with all authority and power.

Rejection will give you greater compassion for others as you allow God's love to be released within you. Through rejection you learn forgiveness. As you release the hurt, you allow more room for God's love to be poured freely within your own heart. This enables you to forgive and love others who have rejected you. God's love is far greater than any of your past rejections. Coming to know the love of God will enable you to override negative human emotion toward others. Paul charges you to strive to comprehend God's love in Ephesians 3:17-19, "So that Christ may dwell in your hearts through faith; and that you, being rooted and grounded in love, may be able to comprehend with all the saints what is the breadth and length and height and depth, and to know the love of Christ with surpasses knowledge, that you may be filled up to all the fullness of God."

From Pain to Purpose

Keep in mind that although you may have been rejected by someone, most likely, you have also rejected someone in your past. So do not expect others to be perfect; just love them for who they are and Christ will do the rest. Jesus loved you even when you rejected Him. He expects the same of you regarding others. Allow Christ to continually reveal aspects of His undying love towards you as you release past rejections. Just watch Him turn your rejection into His correction.

Pain to Propel

God does not plan for pain to be your end point, but your beginning point into your divine destiny. Jesus endured pain on the cross beyond what you can ever imagine as the beginning point for your complete deliverance. His pain has propelled you to walk in love, godliness, supernatural blessings, prosperity, and to inherit eternal life. Through Christ, your past pain will propel you into your divine future without looking back.

You do not have to live in your past. Paul tells us in Philippians 3:

> Not that I have already obtained all this, or have already been made perfect, but I press on to take hold of that for which Christ Jesus took hold of me. Brother, I do not consider myself yet to have taken hold of it. But one thing I do: Forgetting what is behind and straining toward what is ahead, I press on toward the goal to win the prize for which God has called me heavenward in Christ Jesus.
>
> —Philippians 3:12–14, niv

Jesus will use what you thought destroyed you and moved you backward to actually propel you forward into a successful future. The things that previously hurt you begin to help you. This will enable you to minister to other women what God has done for you. Once Jesus changes your life with His healing touch, it will propel you to help others. This is exactly what several women did after they had an encounter with Jesus:

> After this, Jesus traveled about from one town and village to another, proclaiming the good news of the kingdom of God. The Twelve were with him, and also some women who had been cured of evil spirits and diseases: Mary (called Magdalene) from whom seven demons had come out; Joanna the wife of Cuza, the manager of Herod's household; Susanna; and many others. These women were helping to support them out of their own means.
> —Luke 8:1–3, niv

Pain can affect anyone. The beauty of it is Jesus can heal anyone. His healing power will draw women together from various backgrounds for the purpose of following Him to touch the lives of others. This carries you out of your comfort zone into a divine journey. When you are in His divine will, nothing happens in your life just by coincidence.

Your divine journey was already planned before you were born. God already knew that you would experience these painful encounters. Therefore, He devised a plan to incorporate them into the components, which will propel you into your destiny. He uses your past pain to encourage, comfort, and motivate others through what He has done in your life. In other words, your past pain will help others gain understanding of God's purpose for their lives. He truly will transform pain into gain through His divine purpose.

CHAPTER 5

Arise, My Daughter

Has your alarm clock ever gone off early in the morning at a time when you did not feel like getting up? You could have easily stayed in bed with the curtains drawn and the blinds closed for several more hours if it were your choice, right? Although it may seem ideal to be able to do this whenever you like, staying in this mode too long would not be healthy. Think of all you would be missing. First of all, in a dark room you could not see the brightness of the day. Secondly, you would not be involved in outside activities. Finally, you could not proceed with your daily responsibilities. You would no longer be in motion or circulation with the lives of others. You would become stagnant.

What once may have seemed like a comfort zone could now be a death zone in your life. Death zones are the hopeless areas in your life that have been that way for so long that it may seem impossible to you for new life to develop in these areas. Death zones are dark and stagnant without life. Where there is no life source, there is no light. On the contrary, Jesus is life and in His presence death and darkness cannot remain. Therefore, you do not have to dwell in a death mode, but arise to the position that Jesus is calling you to. The alarm clock has gone off for too long now. Your hour has come. He is calling you to arise just as He did a little girl:

> And when Jesus had recrossed in the boat to the other side, a great throng gathered about Him, and He was at the lakeshore. Then one of the rulers of the synagogue came up, Jarius by name; and seeing Him, he prostrated himself at His feet and begged Him earnestly, saying, My little daughter is at the point of death. Come and lay Your hands on her, so that she may be healed and live. And Jesus went with him....When they arrived at the house of the ruler of the synagogue, He looked [carefully and with understanding] at [the] tumult and the people weeping and wailing loudly. And when He had gone in, He said to them, Why do you make an uproar and weep? The little girl is not dead but is sleeping. And they laughed and jeered at Him. But He put them all out, and, taking the child's father and mother and those who were with Him, He went in where the little girl was lying. Gripping her [firmly] by the hand, He said to her, Talitha cumi—which translated is, Little girl, I say to you, arise [from the sleep of death]! And instantly the girl got up and started walking around—for she was twelve years old. And they were utterly astonished and overcome with amazement.
> —MARK 5:21–24; 38–42, AMP

You may be sleeping through life as a result of past failures, mistakes, and bad experiences. Perhaps others have given up on you and called you dead, but Jesus never gives up. In fact, he will call you back to life with words so powerful that death zones are destroyed. His words translate into: arise from depression, arise from abuse, arise from hopelessness, arise from unhappiness, arise from loneliness, and arise from any defeat of the enemy.

He has called you to wake up out of your old life and arise into a new life of victory. Just as Christ arose from death and

Arise, My Daughter

now sits on the throne at the right hand of the Father with all authority and power, so can you. "But God, being rich in mercy, because of His great love with which He loved us, even we were dead in our transgressions, made us alive together with Christ (by grace you have been saved), and raised us up with Him, and seated us with Him in the heavenly places in Christ Jesus" (Eph. 2:4–6). Ladies, it is time to arise to the occasion and take hold of what already belongs to you. Just listen to the voice of Jesus telling you, "Arise, my daughter."

Dusk to Dawn

As dusk arrives in the evening, darkness sets in and light gradually fades away. Only distorted shadows from street and traffic lights remain. Eventually during the night, everything settles to a complete standstill. The only proof of daylight was the memory of yesterday with the hope of light tomorrow. Have shadowy circumstances fallen on you to the degree that you feel it can never be lifted? Are there dark areas from your past that seem to hold you back? Have you been living in shame or guilt for so long that you feel like it has destroyed any hope of life within you? If so, dusk has gradually settled upon you. Remaining here will leave you lifeless and keep you hopeless.

You must understand that dark circumstances in life will come. However, you must pass through them and not remain in them. Christ will be with you as you walk through these areas. Psalm 23:4 states, "Even though I walk through the valley of the shadow of death, I will fear no evil, for you are with me" (NIV). God does not tell you dark times will not come. He does assure you that the light of dawn will follow.

Therefore, do not settle and get comfortable in the darkness of negative circumstances. Keep moving on because dawn is on the way. Dawn is the point when daylight appears. This is when darkness subsides and obscurity turns into clarity. During the dawn you have clear perception and understanding of things that did not make any sense in the dark. You realize that what appeared to be large scary shadows in the dark were only tiny leaves on a twig.

Satan wants you to remain in the dark so that you cannot gain clear understanding of where you are and where you are going. On the other hand, God created you to be a daughter of light because He is the Father of Light, "Every good thing given and every perfect gift is from above, coming down from the Father of lights, with whom there is no variation or shifting shadow" (James 1:17). God created light out of darkness by His spoken word when He created the heaven and the earth:

> In the beginning God created the heaven and the earth. And the earth was without form, and void; and darkness was upon the face of the deep. And the Spirit of God moved upon the face of the waters. And God said, Let there be light: and there was light. And God saw the light, that it was good: and God divided the light from the darkness. And God called the light Day, and the darkness he called Night. And the evening and the morning were the first day.
> —GENESIS 1:1–5, KJV

You do not have to fear darkness in your life. God has already called light out of it. He has called success out of your failure, joy out of depression, prosperity out of debt, peace out of torment, and victory out of defeat! Weeping may have endured for a night, but joy is coming because the light of dawn is arising. (See Psalm 30:5.)

GET UP AND GO, GIRL!

Let us retrace the previous scenario when the alarm clock went off early in the morning and you did not feel like getting up. Well, get up anyway! Morning has finally arrived so you must arise out of sleep and get on with your divine destiny. You can-

Arise, My Daughter

not fulfill your divine purpose if you remain asleep. Ephesians 5:14 states, "For this reason it says, 'Awake, sleeper, and arise from the dead, and Christ will shine on you.'" Christ is waiting to shine His glory on you so that you can shine within this lost and dying world as a witness for Him:

> Arise, shine, for your light has come, and the glory of the Lord rises upon you. See, darkness covers the earth and thick darkness is over the peoples, but the Lord rises upon you and his glory appears over you. Nations will come to your light, and kings to the brightness of your dawn.
> —Isaiah 60:1–3, niv

You waited too long for the brightness of day to come to remain in darkness. It is time to get up and go, girl! Go after your God-given dream. Once you are out in the light, you gain crystal-clear understanding and direction to your destiny. The light uncovers all of your gifts, talents, and abilities to become a woman of success.

Your birth was not a mistake. Before you were even conceived God had already planned your destiny. He deposited these gifts, talents, and abilities deep within you to enable you to soar high above a life of mediocrity. You were not created to blend in with everyone else. You were created to shine bright and to stand out as His elect.

You must use godly wisdom to prepare yourself to arise when He calls you. You must not get so preoccupied with other cares that you are not prepared to get up and go with Jesus. Moreover, do not allow what you see others doing to get you off focus. Let us explore a parable that Jesus told of how five wise women and five foolish women responded to the midnight call:

> THEN THE kingdom of heaven shall be likened to ten virgins who took their lamps and went to meet the bride-

groom. Five of them were foolish (thoughtless, without forethought) and five were wise (sensible, intelligent, and prudent). For when the foolish took their lamps, they did not take any [extra] oil with them; But the wise took flasks of oil along with them [also] with their lamps. While the bridegroom lingered and was slow in coming, they all began nodding their heads, and they fell asleep. But at midnight there was a shout, Behold, the bridegroom! Go out to meet him! Then all those virgins got up and put their own lamps in order. And the foolish said to the wise, Give us some of your oil, for our lamps are going out. But the wise replied, There will not be enough for us and for you; go instead to the dealers and buy for yourselves. But while they were going away to buy, the bridegroom came, and those who were prepared went in with him to the marriage feast; and the door was shut.
—Matthew 25:1–10, amp

Do not allow foolishness or laziness to keep you asleep, unmotivated, and unprepared to get up and enter into your divine destiny. Satan wants to stall you by any possible means to keep you down, depressed, and distressed. Satan realizes that timing is everything with respect to your wake-up call. Therefore when it is your time to arise and shine, recognize the call, drop everything, and get up and go!

Alive and Well

Once you awaken, arise, and answer the call, you will live a new life like never before. You will be better than ever. You have been revived and restored. You are now walking in the supernatural. Through Him you are living, moving, and having your being. (See Acts 17:28.) Often, Christians struggle in the area of living by the Spirit of God as opposed to living by their carnal nature. Your natural self wants you to behave the way you used to before you arose out of darkness, but the Spirit stirs you up to live supernaturally, shining in the light of His glory.

Arise, My Daughter

The Spirit and the flesh will never agree about your divine destiny. Your flesh will tell you that it can never happen, but the Spirit of God will make it happen. Remain mindful of Paul's teachings regarding the Spirit and the flesh:

> For those who are according to the flesh set their minds on the things of the flesh, but those who are according to the Spirit, the things of the Spirit. For the mind set on the flesh is death, but the mind set on the Spirit is life and peace, because the mind set on the flesh is hostile toward God; for it does not subject itself to the law of God, for it is not even able to do so, and those who are in the flesh cannot please God. However, you are not in the flesh but in the Spirit, if indeed the Spirit of God dwells in you. But if anyone does not have the Spirit of Christ, he does not belong to Him. If Christ is in you, though the body is dead because of sin, yet the spirit is alive because of righteousness. But if the Spirit of Him who raised Jesus from the dead dwells in you, He who raised Christ Jesus from the dead will also give life to your mortal bodies through His Spirit who dwells in you. So then, brethren, we are under obligation, not to the flesh, to live according to the flesh—for if you are living according to the flesh, you must die; but if by the Spirit you are putting to death the deeds of the body, you will live. For those who are being led by the Spirit of God, these are sons of God.
> —ROMANS 8:5–14

A new life in the Spirit involves putting away old mindsets, habits, and inabilities in order to be led by the Spirit. In this realm, there are no limitations or restrictions to what God will do in your life when you trust Him. You see, in order to truly be alive and well you must be led by the Holy Spirit in every area of your life. This means that you no longer steer your own life because the Holy Spirit will direct you.

As you flow with the Spirit, you will gain daily direction

in decision-making, relationships, and new opportunities. Through the Spirit, you will distinguish between what is real or fake, safe or dangerous, and right or wrong. Deep within this innermost part of you, you will sense a peace about something or a red flag. Before you arose out of darkness, you may have received warnings from the Spirit. However, you were not Spirit-controlled and most likely ignored these warnings.

Now that you are alive and well, you will begin singing a new song of honor, praise, and glory to God for what He has done in your life. He will put a new rhythm in your step just like David:

> My heart is steadfast, O God; I will sing, I will sing praises, even with my soul. Awake, harp and lyre; I will awaken the dawn! I will give thanks to You, O LORD, among the peoples, and I will sing praises to You among the nations. For Your lovingkindness is great above the heavens, and Your truth reaches to the skies.
> —PSALM 108:1–4

You have the choice to be alive in Christ or to remain asleep in a death zone of darkness. What will you choose when He calls you— life or death?

> See, I set before you today life and prosperity, death and destruction. For I command you today to love the LORD your God, to walk in his ways, and to keep his commands, decrees and laws; then you will live and increase, and the LORD your God will bless you in the land you are entering to possess. But if your heart turns away and you are not obedient, and if you are drawn away to bow down to other gods and worship them, I declare to you this day that you will certainly be destroyed. You will not live long in the land you are crossing the Jordan to enter and possess. This day I call heaven and earth as witnesses against you that I have set before you life and death,

blessings and curses. Now choose life, so that you and your children may live and that you may love the LORD your God, listen to his voice, and hold fast to him. For the LORD is your life, and he will give you many years in the land he swore to give to your fathers, Abraham, Isaac and Jacob.
—DEUTERONOMY 30:15–20, NIV

The Israelites had to make a choice to follow God into their divine destiny with a life of blessings and prosperity, or sink into darkness and despair. Does it not seem obvious that anyone given this choice would select blessings, security, and safety without hesitating? Unfortunately, this is not always the case. Many people throughout biblical history chose to live outside of God's will, remain in darkness, and worship other gods. Sadly enough, even today people are not answering His call out of darkness. People today may not worship idols carved out of stone or gold, but they worship their careers, education, talents, money, and sports to only mention a few. An idol is any person, object, or position that is more important to you than God.

Perhaps you have not answered His call to arise because you have been too preoccupied with idols to recognize His voice. If God is not your focus, Satan gains latitude into your life to keep you depressed, discouraged, tormented, and distressed. I urge you in the name of Jesus to put Him first and foremost in your life. Become Spirit-controlled and you can never lose. He would not have called you out of death to life for you to fail. I declare unto you that you are alive in Christ Jesus and doing well.

CHAPTER 6

Unfading Beauty

What is beauty? Our society portrays beauty as facial features, body types, hairstyles, makeup, and fashion. Just look around at commercials, billboards, magazines, and shopping malls. Sales of beauty products are at an all time high because women want to look their best. Many times this pressure to have to look a certain way can deter your attention away from your focus, leave you lonely, and make you unapproachable.

This world's view of beauty is quite different from Christ's view of beauty. The world looks at you on the outside. God always looks on the inside. The real you is not what others see by your physical appearance. The real you is what others see coming out from the inside of you. True beauty is the reflection of God's love pouring out from you like the rays of the sun. His love can never fade away or become obsolete.

Women, do not fall into the trap of becoming so preoccupied with your outside appearance that it robs you from your true purpose to glorify God. There is certainly nothing wrong with maintaining physical attractiveness and good health. However, you must always keep God first in your life. The obsession to obtain society's standard of beauty can change your character to vanity, pride, and selfishness. This will actually turn people away from you and leave others hesitant to even approach you. Does this not defeat the purpose of why you sought this type of beauty in the first place? Outer beauty alone may provide a temporary fix, but it will not last long. There must be something more.

Have you ever wondered what attracted the multitudes of people to Jesus when He lived on earth? Thousands of people left their homes and gathered together to see Him, hear Him, and just be near Him. Yes, He performed miracles right before their eyes, but there was more to it than this. They saw love permeating through Him. Perhaps some of them could not explain or pinpoint exactly how He drew them there, but they certainly would not leave. In fact, they remained with Him for several days until they grew rather hungry:

> During those days another large crowd gathered. Since they had nothing to eat, Jesus called his disciples to him and said, "I have compassion for these people; they have already been with me three days and have nothing to eat. If I send them home hungry, they will collapse on the way, because some of them have come a long distance." His disciples answered, "But where in this remote place can anyone get enough bread to feed them?" "How many loaves do you have?" Jesus asked. "Seven," they replied. He told the crowd to sit down on the ground. When he had taken the seven loaves and given thanks, he broke them and gave them to his disciples to set before the people, and they did so. They had a few small fish as well; he gave thanks for them also and told the disciples to distribute them. The people ate and were satisfied. Afterward the disciples picked up seven basketfuls of broken pieces that were left over. About four thousand men were present.
>
> —MARK 8:1–9, NIV

Unfading Beauty

Jesus had a heart of love for people. His actions toward them were demonstrations of His love. True beauty gives out to others to meet their needs. Just as Jesus multiplied fish and bread to feed others, so will His beauty within you multiply to touch the lives of everyone with whom you come into contact. We will explore aspects of inward beauty that will challenge you to a complete makeover and motivate you to utilize some beauty secrets to attain this rare beauty that can never fade away.

THE HEART OF A BEAUTIFUL WOMAN

There seems be a common thread in the hearts of beautiful godly women. Certainly they all differ as individuals; however, their hearts share commonalities. Their actions demonstrate God's love for them, through them, and for others. The heart of a woman will determine what will come out of her. A woman with a pure heart radiates the beauty of God. Her beauty is not based on her outward appearance, but on her inward love and compassion. As a result, beautiful women give, care, and comfort others. Have you ever given something very special of yours away to someone that needed it more than you? Was it a struggle for you? Did you regret giving it away? The heart of a giver offers herself, her time, and her resources to help others in need.

It makes no sense to our society why one would go out of their way to help another. However, it also makes no sense why God gave His only Son, Jesus Christ, as the sacrifice for our sins. He did it because He loves you so deeply. "For God so loved the world, that He gave His only begotten Son, that whoever believes in Him shall not perish, but have eternal life" (John 3:16). You cannot make sense out of love. You act on it.

Because God loved, He gave. As a result, if the love of God is in your heart, you will desire to give. A beautiful woman does not give because she is seeking attention. She gives because she wants to display to others God's love for them. There are many broken and wounded people that have been left by the wayside because no one has taken the time to care. This is where you come into the picture:

> In reply Jesus said: "A man was going down from Jerusalem to Jericho, when he fell into the hands of robbers. They stripped him of his clothes, beat him and went away, leaving him half dead. A priest happened to be going down the same road, and when he saw the man, he passed by on the other side. So too, a Levite, when he came to the place and saw him, passed by on the other side. But a Samaritan, as he traveled, came where the man was; and when he saw him, he took pity on him. He went to him and bandaged his wounds, pouring on oil and wine. Then he put the man on his own donkey, took him to an inn and took care of him. The next day he took out two silver coins and gave them to the innkeeper. 'Look after him,' he said, 'and when I return, I will reimburse you for any extra expense you may have.'"
> —LUKE 10:30–35, NIV

What would you have done under similar circumstances? Would you have just walked in another direction because you had more important things to do with your time? Would you first look around to see if others were watching you? Would the attention of others change your actions? A woman of beauty acts irrespective of various circumstances. A beautiful woman realizes that God knows her heart and sees her actions as a result. Therefore, she desires to please Him in every aspect of her life. This involves having compassion for others and taking that extra time and effort to help others in need. Beauty is what beauty gives.

A Complete Makeover

We commonly associate makeovers with perhaps television shows and fashion magazines involving women with before and after comparisons. Many times these women look completely different after their makeover, leaving their own families and closest friends utterly astonished. Often, these women say afterwards they never thought it was possible to improve their appearance so much, giving credit to the hair stylists, fashion consultants, and makeup artists. What these women do not understand is they always had the potential to look this way. They just needed the help of professionals that were able to bring or draw out the best in them. Similarly, you must understand that you have all the potential you need for a complete spiritual makeover.

You must allow Christ to draw out the best from within you. Remember what He has started in you, He will certainly finish. (See Philippians 1:6.) God already knows the gifts within you. He put them there. Only He is able add a little here, subtract a bit there, and add just the perfect finishing touches. If you only knew your true beauty potential, you would quickly sit in the Master's styling chair and allow Him to begin His work within you. He will beautify every area of your being from the top of your head to the soles of your feet. Sisters, sit back and get ready for a full body makeover.

Eyes

Beautiful eyes see the good in others. They are not looking at others to find faults or imperfections. They do not judge others based how they appear on the outside. These eyes see past someone with a bad attitude or someone that mistreated them. They look to Jesus to gain a clear vision of how He sees others. Beautiful eyes reflect God's genuine love and sincerity for people. They look past present circumstances and trials knowing that they are only temporary and God is preparing them for greatness.

Ears

Beautiful ears take time out of their busy schedule to listen to someone in need. These ears are sensitive to a cry for help. They do not ignore people that others think are unimportant. They do not listen to gossip or draw conclusions based on what they have heard. Beautiful ears listen to the voice of the Holy Spirit for guidance. They are eager to hear the Word of God and quickly put it into action.

Lips

Great lips speak words of kindness regardless of how they are treated by someone. They frequently speak out the Word of God and encourage others through the Word. They are quick to testify about God's goodness. Most importantly, they spread the Good News of Jesus Christ to others. These lips rely on the Holy Spirit to know when to speak and when to remain silent. Perfect lips diligently pray for God's perfect will instead of their own.

Cheeks

Perfect cheeks love their enemies and willingly go out of their way to do good even when they were spitefully wronged. Beautiful cheeks do not get puffed up with anger, but turn away to keep the peace. High cheekbones are tough enough to rise above adversity. These cheeks do not shatter during the storms of life. To the contrary, they allow the storms to restructure them to become beautifully sculptured into a work of art.

Nose

A beautiful nose is not stuck up in the air looking down at others. This nose breathes in good and bad smelling air. In other words, this nose accepts people that smell good and not so good. This nose treats the homeless the same as the famous. A beautiful nose realizes that we are all equal in God's eyes. Instead of sniffing around in others people's business as a busybody, this nose recognizes its own shortcomings and relies on God's mercy.

Skin

Beautiful skin is ageless. This skin is not insecure with wrinkles, scars, or imperfections. It does not judge others by the color of their skin. Beautiful skin is softened by the anointed oil of the Holy Spirit and is cleansed by the blood of Jesus. This skin is penetrated with a sweet-smelling aroma of kindness and goodness. It will take off its own covering to warm another dying in the cold.

Arms

Beautiful arms are long, strong, and flexible. They use their length to reach out to help people in need. These arms are willing to hug, embrace, and hold someone during a crisis. They use their strength to pull someone out of a ditch and firmly guide them to level ground. They use flexibility to go out of their way to help someone. These beautiful arms lift themselves high to worship and praise God for his goodness and grace.

Legs

Great legs are not easy to come by. These legs must bear the weight of the whole body, yet remain functional. They are deeply rooted in the foundation of God. This enables them to keep themselves grounded while holding others up. Strong legs quickly kick away potential threats and disturbances that could bring harm and cause them to collapse. Beautiful legs are firmly toned by exercising God's law of truth, righteousness, and holiness to stand under any circumstance.

THE BEAUTIFUL COMPLETE WOMAN

Women desire to be beautiful in some way or another. God desires that you are beautiful in every way. God is not a halfway God. He does everything with completeness when He is allowed. It is never too late for your complete makeover. He will get to work right away, but only when you are ready. What are you waiting for?

It does not matter whether you are old, young, single, married, or divorced. You are still a candidate to become beautified. What you single women must understand is what makes a beautiful woman also makes a beautiful wife and mother. Remember, you are a woman in preparation for your divine future. Keeping this in mind, we will explore the attributes of a well-known woman of beauty presented in Proverbs 31.

> Who can find a virtuous woman? for her price is far above rubies.
> —Proverbs 31:10, KJV

If such a woman were easy to find, there would be no question regarding who could find her. You see, "virtuous" pertains to goodness, righteousness, and moral excellence. These are qualities more striking than precious jewels. A beautiful woman is priceless.

> She riseth also while it is yet night, and giveth meat to her household, and a portion to her maidens.
> —Proverbs 31:15, KJV

This woman goes out of her way to give and nourish others even when it may be inconvenient for her. She understands the importance of providing spiritual food to those around her to motivate them, strengthen them, and build them up.

> She girdeth her loins with strength, and strengtheneth her arms.
> —Proverbs 31:17, KJV

She is strong and spiritually fit. She regularly exercises prayer and the Word of God. With this strength, she is able to put on the armor of God to equip herself for spiritual warfare.

> She stretcheth out her hand to the poor; yea, she reacheth

Unfading Beauty

forth her hands to the needy.
—Proverbs 31:20, kjv

She is involved in caring, sharing, and giving to those in (emotional, physical, spiritual, or financial) need. She keeps herself readily available for service.

Strength and honor are her clothing; and she shall rejoice in time to come.
—Proverbs 31:25, kjv

She is clothed in the finest. This strength denotes security. This honor denotes that she is held with the utmost respect. Her clothing will never wear out. She can rejoice for her future because she knows that her divine destiny is in the hands of her Heavenly Father.

She openeth her mouth with wisdom; and in her tongue is the law of kindness.
—Proverbs 31:26, kjv

She has spiritual wisdom. This gives her the ability to discern when to speak and when to remain quiet. She is not involved with gossip, but speaks words of kindness to others.

Her children arise up, and call her blessed; her husband also, and he praiseth her.
—Proverbs 31:28, kjv

Her children will grow up acknowledging that their mother is highly favored of God. In addition, her husband will commend her for attaining this rare beauty.

Many daughters have done virtuously, but thou excellest them all.
—Proverbs 31:29, kjv

She is not threatened by other women. She realizes that her beauty is unique and precious to God. This places her in a category of her own. She leaves no room for comparison.

> Favor is deceitful, and beauty is vain; but a woman that feareth the LORD, she shall be praised.
> —PROVERBS 31:30, KJV

Favor in this world relies on charm and manipulation for promotion. However, the favor of God is upon all those who live uprightly before Him. Beauty only skin deep serves little purpose and will eventually fade away. A woman who reverently fears and worships God has attained a beauty that can never fade away with time or circumstances.

BEAUTY SECRETS

Too often, women have kept beauty tips within their own "social circles." As a result, they have remained well-kept secrets that have only benefited a few. These secrets are only beneficial if they truly assist in beautifying someone and if they are revealed to help others. The time has come to unleash some spiritual tips that will change the way you see yourself and how others see you. They are called beauty secrets.

UNCONDITIONAL LOVE

How God sees you should affect and reflect the way you see others. He loves you unconditionally. This means His love will remain for you regardless of what you have done, what you look like, what you have, or where you came from. Likewise, you must carry on with others in the same respect. This type of love will inhibit you from forming elite social "cliques" that only include some women while excluding others.

Unconditional love never says, "I'm too good for _____," or "I'm better than _____." Can you imagine Jesus saying this about you? If He had felt this way, He certainly would not have died on the cross. To the contrary, He loved so deeply that while He was on the cross suffering, He asked God to forgive those who put them there. (See Luke 23:34.) Likewise, continue in this unconditional love, remembering that your inheritance is eternal life. "Keep yourselves in God's love as you wait for the mercy of our Lord Jesus Christ to bring you to eternal life" (Jude 21, NIV).

HUMILITY

Unfortunately, it takes many people far too long to submit to God and understand they can do nothing without Him. Humility is the opposite of pride. Pride relies on self. God will open His ear to those who humble themselves before Him. "O LORD, You have heard the desire of the humble; You will strengthen their heart, You will incline your ear" (Ps. 10:17). On the other hand, He will resist those full of pride. (See Psalm 138:6; James 4:6; 1 Peter 5:5.)

Maintaining a humble heart does not imply weakness by any means. Humble people realize how great God is and how powerless they are without Him. They truly depend on God for their next breath. They know that He is their life supply. Without humility there is self-deception. This causes people to become prideful, high-minded, and haughty. A prideful heart can only lead to disaster. "Before his downfall a man's heart is proud, but humility comes before honor" (Prov. 18:12, NIV).

INTEGRITY

What causes a woman to stand and hold firmly to her deepest values against all adversity? The answer is her integrity. A woman of integrity maintains a sound heart and mind. She relies completely on Jesus Christ. She is whole and complete, lacking nothing. Every part of her being has been perfectly integrated by the hand of Christ, forming a strong and beautiful masterpiece. This woman has literally got it all together. Therefore, she has no need to compromise her moral standards when under pressure.

At some point in your life, your integrity will be tested. Never give up the values that Christ so richly instilled in you. Make a stand for His way or the highway for those pressuring you to compromise. Remember, you are not standing alone. He is the strong foundation always with you. "Nevertheless, the firm foundation of God stands, having this seal, 'The Lord knows those who are His,' and, 'Everyone who names the name of the Lord is to abstain from wickedness'" (2 Tim. 2:19).

Reverent Fear

Reverent fear of God has often been confused with a destructive, intimidating, and traumatizing fear of God. Actually, reverent fear results from your true recognition of His awesomeness. He is the Almighty God, Creator of everything, and Ruler over all. He deserves all glory, honor, and reverent worship. This reverent fear is actually an overwhelming respect for God. It causes a deep incentive to keep your life upright before Him, and is the starting point to gaining godly wisdom and understanding. "The fear of the Lord is the beginning of knowledge; Fools despise wisdom and instruction" (Prov. 1:7).

A wise woman who fears the Lord makes decisions that will set building blocks for her future. She does not participate in self-destructive behaviors. She knows that she was created for His divine purpose. "The wise woman builds her house, but the foolish tears it down with her own hands" (Prov. 14:1). This fear of God guards you from yielding to temptation and becoming lukewarm.

Unfading Beauty

JUST WHOM ARE YOU TRYING TO ATTRACT?

In lieu of this chapter focusing only on beauty, it seems only relevant to discuss exactly whom you are striving to attract with your beauty. You have probably heard the cliché, "Beauty lies in the eye of the beholder," right? With this in mind, ask yourself this question, "Just who will behold my beauty?" Being beautiful and being sexy are completely different. Sexiness involves only arousing sexual or sensual desire in someone. This is no match for godly beauty. God's beauty penetrates His love through you into the hearts of people that do not know Him. This beauty makes you a valuable witness for God to a lost and dying world.

Your beauty should be turning the heads of coworkers, clients, customers, neighbors, and anyone with whom you come into contact. They will see Christ in you. If your goal is only to attract men, then your mind is in the wrong place. Colossians 3:2–5 (NIV) states, "Set your minds on things above, not on earthly things. For you died, and your life in now hidden with Christ in God. When Christ, who is your life, appears, then you also will appear with him in glory. Put to death, therefore, whatever belongs to your earthly nature: sexual immorality, impurity, lust, evil desires and greed, which is idolatry" (NIV). Know what your true beauty was intended for, and His love will do the rest.

CHAPTER 7

Tunnel Vision

Have you ever been in an underground or underwater tunnel? Tunnels are a means of passage through or under barriers. The only two directions to look in a tunnel are ahead or behind. This generated the term *tunnel vision*. It characterizes a narrow visual field in which peripheral vision is completely eliminated. A person with this condition has a narrow focus and an inability to see other distractions. Similarly, you must develop this tunnel vision spiritually in the pursuit of your divine destiny. After God has deposited a vision into your spirit, you must avoid any distraction that can become a barrier and tunnel your focus on the prize.

Spiritual tunnel vision is only effective if you are looking ahead and not behind. God's divine plan lies before you while mistakes, hurts, and failures lie behind you. Looking back will only bring discouragement and weaken your faith. Paul understood the importance of not looking back, "Brethren, I do not regard myself as having laid hold of it yet; but one thing I do: forgetting what lies behind and reaching forward to what lies ahead, I press on toward the goal for the prize of the upward call of God in Christ Jesus" (Phil. 3:13–14). Therefore, keep your focus on what lies ahead and move in that direction, leaving no opportunity for determent.

If your focus is not in alignment with God's divine will, you may find yourself attempting to build your own tunnel in order to pass through the barriers that you will face. The problem with this is that you do not have the power to pass through these obstacles without God. This will overwork you, exhaust you, and leave you utterly fatigued. If you do not have any focus at all, then you are most likely just moving in whatever direction the wind blows. This gives Satan greater latitude in attempting to rob you of your divine destiny. God has already laid your divine future ahead of you. Get your focus in alignment with His and get on with it!

Jesus himself maintained spiritual tunnel vision while He was on earth. His focus was on doing the will of God regardless of the cost. Jesus knew His purpose. Follow me closely through this passage to discover what knowing your purpose entails:

> It was just before the Passover Feast. Jesus knew that the time had come for him to leave this world and go to the Father. Having loved his own who were in the world, he now showed them the full extent of his love. The evening meal was being served, and the devil had already prompted Judas Iscariot, son of Simon, to betray Jesus. Jesus knew that the Father had put all things under his power, and that he had come from God and was returning to God; so he got up from the meal, took off his outer clothing, and wrapped a towel around his waist. After that, he poured water into a basin and began to wash his disciples' feet, drying them with the towel that was wrapped around him.
>
> —JOHN 13:1–5, NIV

Jesus knew who He was, where He was going, the power He had, and His timing. Because He knew His purpose, He main-

Tunnel Vision

tained tunnel vision to complete it. He knew that He would face the challenges of pain and suffering on the cross. Yet, He remained focused for the purpose of bringing you eternal life. He broke through the blockade of sin and death and has made a tunnel for you to follow Him through. Knowing His purpose did not cause Him to look down on others. To the contrary, He served them with greater love. We will now tunnel through these aspects of your divine purpose as you pattern Jesus Christ.

Knowing Who You Are

It may seem silly to ask yourself "Who am I?" However, I challenge you to do it anyway. Knowing your spiritual origin is critical to understanding your purpose. You were created by God in His own image. This indicates favor toward you. The day of your birth denotes God's particular purpose. The coming of Christ, the Messiah, to this earth had been prophesied thousands of years before He actually came. The day He was born had been predetermined by God from the beginning. Like Christ, your birth date was also predetermined. You were not born by accident or chance. You are a daughter of the Almighty God who created heaven and earth. This is who you are.

Like any loving father, God takes pleasure in letting everyone know who His children are. Actually, He keeps a photo album of you engraved in His own hands. "Behold, I have indelibly imprinted (tattooed a picture of) you on the palm of each of My hands" (Isa. 49:16, AMP). He can never forget that you belong to Him. In addition, He promises unlimited blessings to His children that are obedient:

> All these blessings will come upon you and overtake you if you obey the LORD your God: Blessed shall you be in the city, and blessed shall you be in the country. Blessed shall be the offspring of your body and the produce of your ground and the offspring of your beasts, the increase

of your herd and the young of your flock. Blessed shall be your basket and your kneading bowl. Blessed shall you be when you come in, and blessed shall you be when you go out. The LORD shall cause your enemies who rise up against you to be defeated before you; they will come out against you one way and will flee before you seven ways. The LORD will command the blessing upon you in your barns and in all that you put your hand to, and He will bless you in the land which the LORD your God gives you. The LORD will establish you a holy people to Himself, as He swore to you, if you keep the commandments of the LORD your God and walk in His ways.
—DEUTERONOMY 28:2–9

These are the promises of God to His children that follow His commandments. Satan does not want you to know who you are as a believer because it completely eradicates his efforts of telling you lies. When you understand who you are, Satan can no longer deceive you with negative thoughts, attitudes, or beliefs that do not line up with God's Word. For this reason, it is of utmost importance to read God's Word, meditate on these scriptures, and carry them deep within your heart.

The Holy Spirit will minister to your spirit that you are a child of God. "The Spirit itself beareth witness with our spirit, that we are the children of God: And if children, then heirs; heirs of God, and joint-heirs with Christ" (Rom. 8:16–17, KJV). This means that as a daughter you have inherited great things from God. No one can take this away from you. You ought to arise and shout aloud praises to God right now! This is who you are.

People allow trials in their lives to reflect a negative perception of who they are. God your Father has made big plans for you. He has put investments into your future. Trials are types of investments that have the ability to turn your life completely around, strengthen you, and make you the woman He has called you to be. Without trials you cannot grow. Actually, the

Tunnel Vision

greater the trial is, the greater your inheritance will become. If you are involved in a trial that seems too great, hold on, trust God, and get ready for your inheritance.

God loves you more than you may ever really understand. However, He will begin to reveal His love to you more and more as you focus on Him. "And I pray that you, being rooted and established in love, may have power, together with all the saints, to grasp how wide and long and high and deep is the love of Christ, and to know this love that surpassed knowledge—that you may be filled to the measure of all the fullness of God" (Eph. 3:17–19, NIV). You are loved by your Father so deeply that He never gives up on you, turns you away, or leaves you alone. This is who you are.

Knowing Where You're Going

There is a certain discomfort in being lost in an unfamiliar place, not knowing which direction to go. For many people this circumstance would cause sheer panic and confusion. Similarly, a lack of spiritual direction can bring about spiritual upheaval. However, tunnel vision will enable you to focus in one direction and move accordingly without becoming lost. Tunnel vision will not direct you by what you see with your physical eyes. It relies completely on your spiritual eyes. Peter was able to walk on water toward Jesus as long as he focused on Him. The moment that Peter began to look around, he lost his focus and began to sink. (See Matthew 14:28–31.) If Jesus is your focal point, you will be able to walk over impossible circumstances and continue in the right direction.

What seems to throw people off the right path is their inability to move in only one direction. In today's society you are offered more choices and conveniences than ever before. If you do not like your first choice, you just choose the next and so forth. This world will direct you by what you see, what you hear, what you feel, and what you think. What may have seemed to be a good direction to go yesterday may not seem so good today. Therefore, you conveniently choose a completely different direction in hope that you will somehow end up in the right place. This does not work. "There is a way which seems right to a man, but its end is the way of death" (Prov. 14:12).

God will not lead you by your feelings or your senses. In fact, your emotions do not affect God. He will not operate in this arena. On the other hand, your faith directly affects God. He can only guide you to your divine destiny if you have faith to follow Him. Tunnel vision requires faith in God no matter how bad the circumstances. You must believe that you will reach your destiny. Interestingly, on the road to your destiny, you may encounter people going backwards, some stagnant, and others discouraging you. However, you must continue moving in God's direction regardless of what everyone else is doing. If you happen to encounter another godly sister going the same direction as you, encourage each other and rejoice together.

Keep moving regardless of the previous wrong turns you made. If you fell down, went backwards, or got sidetracked, it is never too late to turn around. Others may tell you it is too late for you, but God will never tell you this. Are you going to believe what a mere human being tells you over what your Divine Creator says? I pray not. Just keep moving. Your spiritual survival will depend on it.

You are probably familiar with popular TV shows that evaluate whether a particular group of people can survive on a desert island. These people journey through a course of time and events, after which, the ones that have survived are rewarded. Everyone may want the prize, but everyone is not willing to endure hardship during the journey. Your journey is the movement or passage from where you are now to your divine destiny. God will not promise you that your journey will be easy. However, He will provide you with all the necessary tools to survive. Do not begin comparing your tools with

Tunnel Vision

someone else's tools on your journey. God has a unique plan for you and only you. Quit worrying about why He is providing for someone else in a different way than you. Just take what He gives you and go with it.

Your journey is intended to bring you to maturity, to strengthen you, and build a deeper relationship with God. People have mistakenly made this a time of fear, complaining, and unbelief. This is exactly what happened when the Israelites wandered in the wilderness for forty years before they reached the Promised Land. Their journey was much longer than what was necessary. When you lose site of where you're going, then you end up just going in circles getting nowhere. On the other hand, tunneling your vision toward God will lead you down the right path to your destination. Day by day you are coming closer and closer to what may seem impossible. There is a reward with your name on it awaiting you.

You learned in mathematics that the shortest distance between any two points is a straight line. If you go off course and make curves to get from one point to the other, the distance will increase. Similarly, the shortest distance to your divine destiny is to walk the straight and narrow path. Attempting to create your own shortcuts will only slow you down. Keep in mind, God did not create you to fail. He knows that you can accomplish all that He has set before you. Although you cannot see everything that lies ahead, know the direction that you are going and walk therein.

Knowing the Power You Have

God's power begins on the inside of you and yields unimaginable results when it is released. The power that you have is God's ability operating within you to perform things that only He can do. There is no limit to His ability. Therefore, there is no limit to your ability. "Now unto him that is able to do exceedingly abundantly above all that we ask or think, according to the power that worketh in us" (Eph. 3:20, KJV). The power working inside of you can accomplish more than what your mind can fathom. The flipside of this is not having the ability to access this power because you are unaware that you have it. Remember the saying, "Knowledge is power."

When Jesus left the earth after His resurrection, He sent the Holy Spirit to fill you with power. "But you shall receive power (ability, efficiency, and might) when the Holy Spirit has come upon you, and you shall be My witnesses in Jerusalem and all Judea and Samaria and to the ends (the very bounds) of the earth" (Acts 1:8, AMP). His power will make you a witness to the world. This power enables you excel beyond political, racial, financial, and social barriers. His power has a purpose. Your divine destiny is not only about you. It is about the power that He has put within you to witness to, minister to, and deliver others that are captive. Your divine destiny will involve working for the kingdom of God.

Can you now see why Satan does not want you to fulfill your God-given purpose? He knows that when you gain this knowledge about yourself, he will have no foothold. Jesus has given you power over the enemy. "Behold! I have given you authority and power to trample upon serpents and scorpions, and [physical and mental strength and ability] over all the power that the enemy [possesses]; and nothing shall in any way harm you" (Luke 10:19, AMP). This power destroys any fear of failure that the enemy will attempt to put into your mind. "For God hath not given us the spirit of fear; but of power, and of love, and of a sound mind" (2 Tim. 1:7, KJV).

This power gives you the ability to accomplish, complete, perform, overtake, or destroy something that could not be done otherwise without it. You will need this power as you maintain tunnel vision to possess the promises. Knowing who you are and where you are going is only effective in reaching your destiny if you utilize God's power to achieve the impossible. "I pray that the eyes of your heart may be enlightened, so that you

Tunnel Vision

will know what is the hope of His calling, what are the riches of the glory of His inheritance in the saints, and what is the surpassing greatness of His power toward us who believe" (Eph. 1:18–19). This power makes you untouchable and unstoppable. Does this seem too good to be true? Jesus Christ fulfilled His purpose on earth with the power that God had given to Him. Likewise, Christ has made this power available to you. This is no joke, magic trick, or fairy tale. This power is real.

Do you remember during your childhood watching cartoons with superheroes? Usually, there was a struggle between good and evil. Although the evil characters may have seemed powerful, the good characters exerted the most power and always prevailed. Similarly, in pursuing your divine purpose, you will have trials. Satan will do everything in his power to get you off track. However, all of his power is incomparable to the power of God within you. When you have this knowledge, it changes your self-perception from being a powerless wimp to being powerful woman of God.

Do not waste your time trying to figure out what obstacles lie ahead and what Satan will do next. Instead, take the authority that you have been given to destroy any stronghold that stands in your way. "The weapons we fight with are not the weapons of the world. On the contrary, they have divine power to demolish strongholds" (2 Cor. 10:4, NIV). Remember, God would not have given you a divine destiny without divine power to achieve it. With this power you will prevail.

Knowing Your Timing

Timing is of utmost importance for the development of any life source. For instance, with the development of an unborn fetus, each week of the pregnancy yields new formation of vital organs and other essential components for life. Consider the four seasons: spring, summer, fall, and winter. The growth and development of crops, flowers, trees, and grass are dependent upon a season of timing. For example, during springtime, you can expect to see leaves budding, birds chirping, and bright green grass. It is a natural progression of development based on what God had already commanded when He created the earth. His commands can never change because they were birthed out of spiritual laws. Natural progression of timing is actually the outward expression of what was already commanded in the spiritual realm.

God has strategically set up your timing into your divine destiny. However, if you do not recognize what is taking place within the supernatural realm, the natural progression may seem too slow, too difficult, or just impossible. This outward progression may not come to pass how and when you think it ought to, but with time it will come. You will see your vision come forth and receive the promise. However, all of these aspects are time-dependent. They will take place during a particular timing in your life that God has already set.

Naturally, this question is probably arising in your mind, "OK, so how do I know when my timing is?" The only way to know the mysteries of God and things that will take place is to stay connected with the Holy Spirit. "But when He, the Spirit of Truth (the Truth-giving Spirit) comes, He will guide you into all the Truth (the whole, full Truth). For He will not speak His own message [on His own authority]; but He will tell whatever He hears [from the Father; He will give the message that has been given to Him], and He will announce and declare to you the things that are to come [that will happen in the future]" (John 16:13, AMP). God will only reveal to you what He desires for you to know. You cannot make Him tell you anything. However, if you maintain tunnel vision, He will deposit a sense of your timing into your spirit. He may not tell you the exact day and hour, but you will sense your season.

Let's look at springtime again. This is the time when dandelions blossom. You do not know the exact day of the week they will bloom, but you do know they will because it is their

Tunnel Vision

season. Because you know that dandelions were created to blossom during springtime, you do not waste time questioning why this is so. Rather, you just expect to see their manifestation during their season. Likewise, you can expect to see a divine manifestation during your season as well.

A common problem is that many women tend to confuse their season with someone else's season. They may see other women being blessed at a certain time so they assume that it must be their timing also. However, you must remember that your divine destiny has its own timing. When your timing does come, you must take full advantage of your season. This is the time to use all that you have to get what you never had. Let's look at a woman who did exactly this:

> Now one of the Pharisees invited Jesus to have dinner with him, so he went to the Pharisee's house and reclined at the table. When a woman who had lived a sinful life in that town learned that Jesus was eating at the Pharisee's house, she brought an alabaster jar of perfume, and as she stood behind him at his feet weeping, she began to wet his feet with her tears. Then she wiped them with her hair, kissed them and poured perfume on them....Then he turned toward the woman and said to Simon, "Do you see this woman? I came into your house. You did not give me any water for my feet, but she wet my feet with her tears and wiped them with her hair. You did not give me a kiss, but this woman, from the time I entered, has not stopped kissing my feet. You did not put oil on my head, but she has poured perfume on my feet. Therefore, I tell you, her many sins have been forgiven—for she loved much. But he who has been forgiven little loves little." Then Jesus said to her, "Your sins are forgiven".... Jesus said to the woman, "Your faith has saved you; go in peace."
>
> —LUKE 7:36–50, NIV

Single But Not Alone

This woman knew her timing and she took full advantage of the opportunity with all she had to pursue her divine destiny. This woman was not perfect but her timing was. It was her time for a new beginning. Know your timing, take advantage of your opportunity, and watch the manifestation unfold.

CHAPTER 8

Strength in Turmoil

IN ORDER TO effectively endure turmoil in life, you must maintain inner strength. This inner strength can only come from God. Too often, turmoil is dealt with ineffectively because people do not rely on God for strength. Trials, tribulations, and calamites can seem like fierce tornados. Do you know people that have faced major catastrophic events? Did you wonder how they endured it? Negative circumstances such as these reveal where your inner-strength lies. If you are not grounded on the right foundation, this turmoil can shatter you completely.

On the other hand, if you are grounded in Christ, He will deposit strength into your spirit. "For this cause I bow my knees unto the Father of our Lord Jesus Christ, of whom the whole family in heaven and earth is named, that he would grant you, according to the riches of his glory, to be strengthened with might by his Spirit in the inner man; that Christ many dwell in your hearts by faith; that ye, being rooted and grounded in love, may be able to comprehend with all saints what is the breadth, and length, and depth, and height; and to know the love of Christ, which passeth knowledge, that ye might be filled with all the fullness of God" (Eph. 3:14–19,

KJV). Paul prayed this for other Christians to endure hardship and know the love of God. Your ability to love others while enduring hardship will determine the magnitude of the blessing that awaits you at the end.

Periods of turmoil will require that you wait on God and draw strength from Him. "Do you not know? Have you not heard? The Everlasting God, the LORD, the Creator of the ends of the earth does not become weary or tired. His understanding is inscrutable. He gives strength to the weary, and to him who lacks might He increases power. Though youths grow weary and tired, and vigorous young men stumble badly, yet those who wait for the LORD will gain new strength; They will mount up with wings like eagles, they will run and not get tired, they will walk and not become weary" (Isa. 40:28–31). You must continue to develop an intimacy with God in order to maintain strength during adversity.

This intimacy generates as a result of spending time in a secret place in the presence of God. "HE WHO dwells in the secret place of the Most High shall remain stable and fixed under the shadow of the Almighty [Whose power no foe can withstand]" (Ps. 91:1, AMP). We will explore how a woman of God made this her dwelling place in the midst of turmoil:

> Now there came a day when Elisha passed over to Shunem, where there was a prominent woman, and she persuaded him to eat food. And so it was, as often as he passed by, he turned in there to eat food. She said to her husband, "Behold now, I perceive that this a holy man of God passing by us continually. "Please let us make a little walled upper chamber and let us set a bed for him there, and a table and a chair and a lampstand; and it shall be, when he comes to us, that he can turn in there." One day he came there and turned in to the upper chamber and rested. Then he said to Gehazi his servant, "Call this Shunammite." And when he called her, she stood before him. He said to him, "Say now to her, 'Behold, you have

Strength in Turmoil

been careful for us with all this care; what can I do for you?....And Gehazi answered, "Truly she has no son and her husband is old." He said, "Call her." When he had called her, she stood in the doorway. Then he said, "At this season next year you will embrace a son." And she said, "No, my lord, O man of God, do not lie to your maidservant." The woman conceived and bore a son at that season the next year, as Elisha had said to her. When the child was grown, the day came that he went out to his father to the reapers. He said to his father, "My head, my head." And he said to his servant, "Carry him to his mother." When he had taken him and brought him to his mother, he sat on her lap until noon, and then died. She went up and laid him on the bed of the man of God, and shut the door behind him and went out.

—2 Kings 4:8–21

The Shunammite woman built a place for a man of God to dwell. You will later see how this in turn gave her strength in the time of turmoil to press on until her victory came forth. She is a prime example of how one maintains strength in turmoil. We will explore how her experience can help guide you to your breakthrough.

Building Your Ark

You obtain direct intimacy with God through a covenant relationship with Him. The Ark of the Covenant was built in the days of Moses as a representation of the sacred covenant between God and His people. His high presence would dwell wherever the ark was. The construction of the ark required the use of tedious skills through wisdom and understanding from God. The people built the ark as God had commanded them. God did not build the ark Himself. Likewise, when the Shunammite woman recognized that the presence of God was with Elisha, she built a room for him to dwell. She welcomed his presence. She sought a covenant relationship with God through Elisha. Therefore, she built this room and put in a bed, a table, a lamp stand, and a chair. Similarly, Moses built a tabernacle to house the ark. A table, lamp stand, and a mercy seat were placed on top of the ark.

> Moses erected the tabernacle and laid its sockets, and set up its boards, and inserted its bars and erected its pillars. He spread the tent over the tabernacle and put the covering of the tent on top of it, just as the LORD had commanded Moses. Then he took the testimony and put it into the ark, and attached the poles to the ark, and put the mercy seat on top of the ark. He brought the ark into the tabernacle, and set up a veil for the screen, and screened off the ark of the testimony, just as the LORD had commanded Moses. Then he put the table in the tent of meeting on the north side of the tabernacle, outside the veil....Then he placed the lampstand in the tent of meeting, opposite the table, on the south side of the tabernacle. He lighted the lamps before the LORD, just as the LORD had commanded Moses....Then he set up the veil for the doorway of the tabernacle. He set the altar of burnt offering before the doorway of the tabernacle of the tent of meeting, and offered on it the burnt offering and the meal offering, just as the LORD had commanded Moses....He erected the court all around the tabernacle and the altar, and hung up the veil for the gateway of the court. Thus Moses finished the work. Then the cloud covered the tent of meeting, and the glory of the LORD filled the tabernacle. Moses was not able to enter the tent of meeting because the cloud had settled on it, and the glory of the LORD filled the tabernacle.
> —EXODUS 40:18–35

The same high presence of God that was with Moses to endure the journey through the wilderness seeking the Promised Land was also with the Shunammite woman seeking res-

Strength in Turmoil

urrection for her son. They both sought the presence of God through an intimate relationship with Him using the necessary tools to build this relationship. Likewise, in order for you to obtain inner strength through the presence of God, you must also build your ark.

How do you build your ark? You must first build Him a room for His presence to dwell. Because your body is the temple of the Holy Ghost, you must give your body to Him as a dwelling place. "Do you not know that your body is the temple (the very sanctuary) of the Holy Spirit Who lives within you, Whom you have received [as a Gift] from God? You are not your own, You were bought with a price [purchased with a preciousness and paid for, made His own]. So then, honor God and bring glory to Him in your body" (1 Cor. 6:19-20, AMP). You must keep your body holy before Him. This means abstaining from a sinful lifestyle. You may give up certain relationships, types of music, movies, social gatherings, and unhealthy habits. God cannot dwell where there is no space for Him.

When God has made a covenant with you, there is an agreement or exchange that takes place between you and God that you will live according to His standards. If you have other idols (anything that takes preference over God) in your life, there can be no covenant. "What agreement [can there be between] a temple of God and idols? For we are the temple of the living God; even as God said, I will dwell in and with and among them and will walk in and with and among them, and I will be their God, and they shall be My people. So, come out from among [unbelievers], and separate (sever) yourselves from them, says the Lord, and touch not [any] unclean thing; then I will receive you kindly and treat you with favor, And I will be a father to you, and you shall be My sons and daughters, says the Lord Almighty" (2 Cor. 6:16-18, AMP). You see, there is a price to building an intimate relationship with God. You have probably heard people say they are, "Keepin' it real." However, with God you must adapt to "Keepin' it holy."

The bed

The Shunammite woman put in a bed for the prophet of God as a resting place for him when he came to town. In like manner, you must add a bed in your temple. This bed represents an altar. Most people do not open their homes to just any guest whenever they come into town. A strong relationship of trust must exist. Moses built an altar as a means to offer sacrifices to God. The Shunammite women laid her dead son on the bed or an altar. "The Lord will sustain, refresh, and strengthen him on his bed of languishing; all his bed You [O Lord] will turn, change, and transform in his illness" (Ps. 41:3, AMP). Coming to an altar and leaving all that is important to you is an act of surrender. The storms of life will lead you to an altar surrendering everything over to Him. You must sacrifice things that you thought were important in order to obtain what you never had. A sacrifice must be consumed before it can have value with God and yield blessings.

The table

The Shunammite woman put a table in the room most likely as an apparatus to place certain necessities such as food and drink. Moses set up a table in the tabernacle with dishes and plates for showbread and pitchers for pouring out drink offerings. He set the arrangement of these items just as God told him. This table represents a means of opportunity to serve God. When you prepare a table for Him, He will indeed prepare a table for you in the presence of trouble and overflow your cup. "You prepare a table before me in the presence of my enemies. You anoint my head with oil; my cup overflows" (Ps. 23:5, NIV). Yes, these are the benefits of setting His table.

The lamp stand

The Shunammite woman put in a lamp stand or candlestick as a means of bringing light to the room. Moses placed a lamp stand or candlestick in the tabernacle and lighted the lamps. A candle only brings light when it is lighted. Similarly,

Strength in Turmoil

the Word of God will bring light to any circumstance in your life if you apply it. "The entrance and unfolding of Your words give light; their unfolding gives understanding (discernment and comprehension) to the simple" (Ps. 119:130, AMP). If you read, study, and meditate on the Word, you will have an understanding of it.

The chair

The Shunammite woman put in a chair for the man of God as an alternative to the bed. Moses placed the mercy seat on top of the ark in the tabernacle. This represents a place of mercy. Where the bed was an altar of surrender and sacrifice, the chair or mercy seat places you in the presence of God's mercy and grace. "Let us therefore come boldly unto the throne of grace, that we may obtain mercy, and find grace to help in time of need" (Heb. 4:16, KJV). His mercy takes no account of your mistakes, shortcomings, or weaknesses. You can sit down in the mercy seat with confidence and assurance that He is truly your help during turmoil.

IT IS WELL

After the Shunammite woman placed her dead son on the bed, she called her husband to ask him for a servant and a donkey to carry her to the man of God:

> Then she called to her husband and said, "Please send me one of the servants and one of the donkeys, that I may run to the man of God and return." He said, "Why will you go to him today? It is neither new moon nor Sabbath." And she said, "It will be well." Then she saddled a donkey and said to her servant, "Drive and go forward; do not slow down the pace for me unless I tell you." So she went and came to the man of God to Mount Carmel. When the man of God saw her at a distance, he said to Gehazi his servant, "Behold, there is the Shunammite. Please run now to meet her and say to her, 'Is it well

with you? Is it well with your husband? Is it well with the child?'" And she answered, "It is well."

—2 KINGS 4:22–26

When he questioned why she wanted to do this, she answered him, "It will be well." Later, when she found the man of God, he asked how she, her husband, and her son were doing. She answered, "It is well." Despite the fact that her son was dead, she was confident that God was going to work it out. Has anyone ever asked you, Why are you still not married? Why are you not making more money? Why are your family members not saved? Why are you still working at the same job? Why have you not started your own business? Why have you not gotten your book published? Just tell them, "It is well."

Why did this woman have such an assurance that God had already worked everything out? Before she became pregnant, Elisha told his servant to call her and she stood in the doorway of the bedroom. She did not enter. She had already built a room, added a bed, table, lamp stand, and a chair. However, she did not go beyond the doorway to enter the room until the day that she laid her dead son on the bed.

Going beyond the veil represents entering into a holy place. Moses set up a veil for the doorway of the tabernacle. The glory of the Lord filled this tabernacle. His very presence was inside of the temple. Because the Shunammite woman had now gone beyond the veil, passing the doorway into the intimate presence of God, she knew that He would make everything well. Because you are the temple of the Holy Ghost, you also have direct access to His presence in the midst of your turmoil.

You enter through the doorway into His presence via the Holy Spirit. You have the choice to either just stand at the doorway or to pass beyond the veil to lay your burdens on the altar. When you go beyond the veil, you pass into a higher intimacy with God. Through prayer, you gain an assurance that it is well. Prayer carries you into the direct presence of God.

Strength in Turmoil

Because your body is the temple of the Holy Spirit, you can now access God directly. This entails getting alone with just you and God.

Family and friends can certainly be a support during turmoil in your life, but your strongest support can only come from God. Only He has the ability to fill you with strength to continue on. King David certainly understood this: "In the day when I called you, You answered me; and You strengthened me with strength (might and inflexibility to temptation) in my inner self" (Ps. 138:3, AMP). Prayer involves calling on the Lord in time of need, praising and worshipping God, or just remaining still and quiet and listening to what He tells you.

As with maintaining communication in any relationship, prayer involves work on your part. Remember, the Shunammite woman built a room for Elisha. She actually did something rather than waiting for someone else to do it. You cannot just wait for others to pray you through distress. You must make the effort to enter His presence for yourself. When God sees your desire to draw near to Him, He will act. "Draw near to God and He will draw near to you. Cleanse your hands, you sinners; and purify your hearts, you double-minded" (James 4:8). As a result of your closeness to Him, your faith increases. "It is well" is a faith statement. It takes no consideration how bad the circumstances may appear before your eyes.

In addition to prayer and faith, you must be obedient to God's commands for all to be will with you. "How blessed is everyone who fears the LORD, who walks in His ways. When you shall eat of the fruit of your hands, you will be happy and it will be well with you" (Ps. 128:1–2). Your obedience activates miracles. "Hear, O Israel, and be careful to obey so that it may go well with you and that you may increase greatly in a land flowing with milk and honey, just as the LORD, the God of your fathers, promised you" (Deut. 6:3, NIV). Being well with you involves what is good, complete, in proper manner, affluent, satisfactory, fortunate, and advantageous. This is promised to you by God. Therefore, when turmoil hits your life, speak out His promises like the Shunammite woman.

Elisha promised this woman that she would give birth to a child that she did not ask him for. Actually, she told him not to lie to her with such a promise. You see, God knows your deepest desires and has blessings awaiting you that you have never asked Him for. The miracle of having this child was beyond what she ever dreamed. However, although she did have the child, the battle was not over. People often think that battles are over after the first miracle comes. If God can work one miracle, He can work multiple miracles. Just because your miracle may appear dead, it is not over until God says it is over.

Breakthrough

When the Shunammite woman went to Elisha after her son died, she reminded him of the time when he promised her this son. Sometimes, when you come to God for a miracle, you have to remind Him of what He has promised you. Certainly, He cannot forget what He told you, but this demonstrates to Him your faith and endurance. This woman knew death could not come between God, herself, and her miracle:

> When she came to the man of God to the hill, she caught hold of his feet. And Gehazi came near to push her away; but the man of God said, "Let her alone, for her soul is troubled within her; and the LORD has hidden it from me and has not told me." Then she said, "Did I ask for a son from my lord? Did I not say, 'Do not deceive me?'".... The mother of the lad said, "As the LORD lives and as you yourself live, I will not leave you." And he arose and followed her....When Elisha came into the house, behold the lad was dead and laid on his bed. So he entered and shut the door behind them both and prayed to the LORD. And he went up and lay on the child, and put his mouth on his mouth and his eyes on his eyes and his hands

Strength in Turmoil

on his hands, and he stretched himself on him; and the flesh of the child became warm. Then he returned and walked in the house once back and forth, and went up and stretched himself on him; and the lad sneezed seven times and the lad opened his eyes. He called Gehazi and said, "Call the Shunammite." So he called her. And when she came in to him, he said, "Take up your son." Then she went and fell at his feet and bowed to the ground, and she took up her son and went out.
—2 KINGS 4:27–37

What does it take for a breakthrough? You trusted God, you were obedient and faithful, and you built a dwelling place for Him. You have done all that you can. What now? The Shunammite woman did all of the above until it was no longer in her hands. After she arrived to where Elisha was at Mount Carmel, she caught him by the foot. When his servant tried to pull her away, he told his servant to leave her alone because her soul was troubled within her. This meant that her soul was rumbled, bothered, annoyed, irritated, shaken up, or put into discomfort. She never actually told Elisha that her son was dead. She only reminded him of his promise to her of having this son. As a result, he immediately took action on her behalf to get to her son.

In order for your breakthrough to come forth, there must be such a rumbling, irritation, or shaking up within your inner self that your present circumstances are no longer acceptable. You have already built an intimate relationship with God and laid your burden at the altar. In other words, you have already gone to a higher spiritual place to see the blessings that belong to you. However, you have not seen any physical manifestation. When your spiritual blessings become so close to being physically manifested, a troubling stirs up within you. Before you can even tell God that your miracle appears dead, He already recognizes the troubling within you. This signals to

Him that it is breakthrough time.

A breakthrough is the actual point where the spiritual promises meet the physical manifestations. Many people confuse this inner troubling with having a lack of faith or a sense of giving up. To the contrary, during this time, the promises are arriving from the spiritual realm and are being transformed into the natural realm. As a result of this transformation process, your inner self can no longer tolerate your present circumstances. When the Shunammite woman arrived at this troubling point, a breakthrough had to come forth.

Elisha followed the Shunammite woman back to her house to the room that she built for him where the boy laid dead on his bed. Your breakthrough may come from the place where you sought His presence from the beginning. Do not try to get your breakthrough in a room that your neighbor built. You must build your own relationship with God. He remembers this secret place is where you served Him, studied His Word, worshiped Him, depended on His mercy, and kept your body a holy temple for Him. It is from this place that the breakthrough is birthed. Everybody wants a breakthrough. However, everyone is not willing to build a place for Him to dwell. Are you willing?

Elisha went into the room where the child was lying dead and shut the door behind him. The Shunammite woman was not in the room with them. After she brought the man of God back, her job was finished. She had reached her endpoint. Once you have done all that you can, God will finish the work. You do not need to worry about how God is going to do it. All that you have to do at this point is to simply wait.

After the child was resurrected, he sent for the Shunammite woman, and told her to take her son. Before she took her son, she fell at Elisha's feet and bowed to the ground. She honored and glorified God for His awesome power and magnificence. After a breakthrough has been manifested, only God can receive the glory. Human beings are not capable of

Strength in Turmoil

performing breakthroughs alone. Therefore, there will be no doubt that the hand of God has broken through what seemed impossible. Sadly enough, people limit themselves by the situations in their lives that seem impossible. However, impossible circumstances are the building blocks to a breakthrough. Unfortunately, these building blocks are often mistaken for roadblocks.

Roadblocks are the things that prevent you from proceeding forward. Building blocks are the things that enable you to proceed forward. Picture yourself driving down a street and you are unable to get any further due to a roadblock. Usually you have to detour via another route to get through to your destination. God does not intend for you to attempt detouring from His plan to get a breakthrough. Unfortunately, people take matters into their own hands to find another route. This will not work. Breakthroughs require supernatural intervention.

Now, picture yourself on the same road. What appeared to be roadblocks were actually the necessary materials that were being used to pave a new street. After this road was constructed, it could carry you to your destination. A nearby construction sign offers you the choice to only wait momentarily while the work is being completed or take a detour completely out of the way. Does it not seem much simpler to just wait for a short time to get through to where you need to go? You will face times in your life when only a breakthrough will get you where God wants you go. We will now discuss some practical steps in identifying the right signal to proceed, when to accelerate, and arriving to the breaking point.

Green Light

A green light is a universal signal to go forward. God expects you to be watchful during this time to recognize your go signal. Too many people are trying to get to a breakthrough on a red light. If everyone drove through red lights, collisions and confusion would result. The same principle applies with spiritual laws. When God signals a green light to you, He has completely cleared the way for you. A green light does not mean proceed slowly with caution. It means, "go." Do not fear that this seems too good to be true and just remain still at a green light. God could be using you as a means to someone else's breakthrough. If you do not move, you could be holding up others that are following you.

Acceleration

This is the process of increasing the speed and intensity of your actions when penetrating through your circumstances. Once you have left the green light you will need to know how fast to go and at what point to speed up. God will actually deposit into your spirit what your next action should be. This could mean spending more time in prayer and fasting.

Breaking Point

The breaking point demonstrates that God has completed the work that He intended. There will be no question, "Is it over yet?" You will know that it is over. You will actually see a miracle manifested. This is the endpoint of what previously seemed impossible. This will be a testimony of what God has done in your life. He must receive the glory for your breakthrough. This entire trial was meant to bring you closer to God for spiritual maturity. Give God all honor, praise, and glory for what He has done and what He will continue to do. Remember, this experience has strengthened you, blessed you, and prepared you for your next challenge.

CHAPTER 9

Courage Above Defeat

OUR SOCIETY REGARDS any action that puts one's own life at stake to save another as an act of courage. We saw such actions during the September 11, 2001 terrorist attack. Brave men and women went beyond the call of duty in some cases to save one person; in other cases, masses of people and ultimately our country as a whole. Regardless of each individual circumstance, some courageous person was willing to act for the behalf of someone else. Does this remind you of what Christ did for you? He died on the cross for your behalf. He defeated the enemy forever. When He died on the cross, He bore our pain, suffering, disease, and sin. This took the burden away from you. In addition to giving up His life for you, He felt every stronghold that came with it. This was the ultimate act of courage.

It would be impossible to defeat the enemy without courage. If you do not defeat Satan, he will attempt to defeat you. Therefore, you must follow after Jesus and courageously defeat Satan's strategies to destroy to you. The fact that you have received a breakthrough will not stop Satan from looking for any opportunity to defeat you. If anything, this makes you a prime target on his hit list. "Be well balanced (temperate, sober of mind), be vigilant and cautious at all times; for that enemy of yours, the devil, roams around like a lion roaring [in fierce hunger], seeking someone to seize upon and devour. Withstand him; be firm in faith [against his onset—rooted, established, strong, immovable, and determined], knowing that the same (identical) sufferings are appointed to your brotherhood (the whole body of Christians) throughout the world" (1 Pet. 5:8–9, AMP). Remember through Christ you have already defeated Satan. It is just a matter of you taking on the boldness of God and keeping Satan under your feet.

Just because God has given you a blessing, you must not become lazy. You cannot afford to just sit and soak up the blessing. You are on a journey to continue moving forward (maturing, advancing, growing) in Christ. Do not let the blessing cause you to stagnate. Instead, use the blessing as an opportunity to save the lives of others. This is exactly what a young Jewish woman did for the sake of her people. Her name is Esther:

> Then the king's attendants, who served him, said, "Let beautiful young virgins be sought for the king. Let the king appoint overseers in all the provinces of his kingdom that they may gather every beautiful young virgin to the citadel of Susa, to the harem, into the custody of Hegai, the king's eunuch, who is in charge of the women; and let their cosmetics be given them. Then let the young lady who pleases the king be queen in place of Vashti." And the matter pleased the king, and he did accordingly. Now there was at the citadel in Susa a Jew whose name was Mordecai…who had been taken into exile from Jerusalem with the captives who had been exiled with Jeconiah king of Judah, whom Nebuchadnezzar the king of Babylon had exiled. He was bringing up Hadassah, that is Esther, his uncle's daughter, for she had no father or mother. Now the young lady was beautiful of form and face, and when her father and mother died, Mordecai

Courage Above Defeat

took her as his own daughter. So it came about when the command and decree of the king were heard and many young ladies were gathered to the citadel of Susa into the custody of Hegai, that Esther was taken to the king's palace into the custody of Hegai, who was in charge of the women. Now the young lady pleased him and found favor with him. So he quickly provided her with her cosmetics and food, gave her seven choice maids from the king's palace and transferred her and her maids to the best place in the harem. Esther did not make known her people or kindred, for Mordecai had instructed her that she should not make them known....Now when the turn of each young lady came to go into King Ahasuerus, after the end of her twelve months under the regulations for the women—for the days of their beautification were completed as follows: six months with oil of myrrh and six months with spices and the cosmetics for women—the young lady would go in to the king in this way: anything that she desired was given her to take with her from the harem to the king's palace....She would not again go in to the king unless the king delighted in her and she was summoned by name. Now when the turn of Esther, the daughter of Abihail the uncle of Mordecai who had taken her as his daughter, came to go in to the king, she did not request anything except what Hegai, the king's eunuch who was in charge of the women, advised. And Esther found favor in the eyes of all who saw her. So Esther was taken to King Ahasuerus to his royal palace in the tenth month which is the month Tebeth, in the seventh year of his reign. The king loved Esther more than all the women, and found favor and kindness with him more than all the virgins, so that he set the royal crown on her head and made her queen instead of Vashti.

—Esther 2:2–17

Esther had been blessed probably beyond what she ever imagined. It would seem that everything would be smooth

109

sailing from this point on. After all, she was married to a king. She was a queen. She was wealthy. Everyone loved her. What more could a girl want? However, God elevates you for a divine purpose. This involves helping, ministering, and saving the spiritual lives of others. Satan will attempt to throw you off focus and out of God's will for your life. Blessings do not exempt you from the enemy's attack. Blessings can attract many challenges. We will unfold how the courage of one woman saved the lives of her people and changed a nation forever.

Chosen

Esther was chosen by King Ahasuerus to become his wife. Why was Esther chosen among all of the other women? God had already made this place for Esther before it was ever thought about. It was only matter of timing. King Ahasuerus was previously married to Vashti until she refused to come in before him at his command to display her beauty among princes and other influential people. As a result, he divorced Vashti. Her royal position was to be replaced by someone better. This is where Esther came in. God chose Esther because He chooses whom He pleases. With the same respect, God chose you also. Your divine position is awaiting you. Only you can fill this position. He will remove someone else to put you in place. When you are chosen, you do not have to work at anything. It is already just yours.

Esther did not choose for King Ahasuerus to divorce his wife and for her to be taken to the palace. It just happened. People that are chosen do not have to plan manipulative schemes to excel. They just walk with ease into God's divine plan. Being chosen is not dependent upon where you are from or what you have. In fact, it really does not make any logical sense at all. Esther was an ordinary girl. Her parents were deceased. She lived in a foreign country that she did not choose to live in. When the king decided to look for another wife, he could have just made a selection among young women only from wealthy influential families. However, he did not. He appointed officers in every province of his kingdom to search out all of these women and bring them in.

When God chooses you, He is not limited by your present circumstances or what seems logical. Favor is not logical. Favor is a manifestation of divine provision. He will favor you among influential people. He will move you right along to where He wants you to be. Esther found favor with Hegai, who was in charge of the women, and he quickly provided her with all that she needed, gave her maids to assist her, and moved her to the best place in the house. Esther did not have this favor because she was beautiful. All of the women there were beautiful. She was given this favor by God to fulfill the destiny that He had for her. He will also do the same for you.

God chose you before this world was ever formed with a divine purpose in mind. "Even as [in His love] He chose us [actually picked us out for Himself as His own] in Christ before the foundation of the world, that we should be holy (consecrated and set apart for Him) and blameless in His sight, even above reproach, before Him in love. For He foreordained us (destined us, planned in love for us) to be adopted (revealed) as His own children through Jesus Christ, in accordance with the purpose of His will [because it pleased Him and was His kind intent]" (Eph. 1:4–5, AMP). You have already been handpicked by God to take part in His purpose. Just knowing this should give you goose bumps. Do not mistakenly think that you are doing God some huge favor because you have a high position. "You did not choose Me but I chose you" (John 15:16). You did not do the choosing. He did. If it had been up to you to choose, you would have chosen people based upon your emotions, logic, and intellect. Sorry, but these have no effect on God.

Esther had to go through twelve months of beauty treatments or purification before she was able to enter into the king's presence. She was already beautiful. However, this process was a regulation for the women. People tell God, "I am ready now and I do not need to go through an additional process." However, being chosen will not exclude you from the time of preparation. This is time of purification to humble and sweeten you for the time ahead. When Esther's time came to go to the king, she did not request to take anything with her except what Hegai, the king's eunuch had suggested. When you are chosen, you must be very careful in whom to rely when making important decisions that can affect your destiny. Take advice from someone with spiritual wisdom regarding your circumstance.

Esther did not only find favor with the King and his servant. She also found favor in the eyes of all who saw her. Your husband may be a part of your divine destiny, but he is not your divine destiny. God has more in store for you that will extend beyond your marriage. He will give you favor with people in all walks of life to pursue His purpose in your life. You will face just as many or more challenges after you are married. You must remain charged up to obtain the courage needed to take on what lies ahead.

Take a Deep Breath

When Esther became queen, her challenges had just begun. She had not revealed to anyone that she was Jewish or that Mordecai was related to her as he advised her. Mordecai found out that two of the king's officials plotted to kill him. He told Esther about this plot. She in turn informed her husband, the king. The two officials were executed. Sometime after this, King Ahasuerus promoted a man named Haman above all of his other leaders. When all of the king's servants bowed down, honored and gave reverence to Haman, Mordecai refused to do so:

> When Haman saw Mordecai neither bowed down nor paid homage to him, Haman was filled with rage. But he disdained to lay hands on Mordecai alone, for they

Courage Above Defeat

had told him who the people of Mordecai were; therefore Haman sought to destroy all of the Jews, the people of Mordecai, who were throughout the whole kingdom of Ahasuerus....Then Haman said to King Ahasuerus, "There is a certain people scattered and dispersed among the peoples in all the provinces of your kingdom; their laws are different from those of all other people and they do not observe the king's laws, so it is not in the king's interest to let them remain. If it is pleasing to the king, let it be decreed that they be destroyed, and I will pay ten thousand talents of silver into the hands of those who carry on the king's business, to put into the king's treasuries." Then the king took his signet ring from his hand and gave it to Haman...the enemy of the Jews. The king said to Haman, "The silver is yours, and the people also, to do with them as you please." Then the king's scribes were summoned on the thirteenth day of the first month, and it was written just as Haman commanded to the king's satraps, to the governors who were over each province and to the princes of each people, each province according to its script, each people according to its language, being written in the name of King Ahasuerus and sealed with the king's signet ring. Letters were sent by couriers to all the king's provinces to destroy, to kill and to annihilate all Jews, both young and old, women and children, in one day, the thirteenth day of the twelfth month...and to seize their possessions as plunder. A copy of the edict to be issued as law in every province was published to all the peoples so that they should be ready for this day.

—ESTHER 3:5–14

As a result of this death warrant of all the Jewish people in that area, the entire city was in complete confusion. Mordecai sent word to Esther of what was going on. Naturally, after finding this out, she became very distressed. Have you ever been so blessed that it seemed as though nothing could ever go wrong? You have a wonderful God-given husband, the kids are doing well, you're making more money than ever before, or you finally got your business up and running. You can look back and see just how far God has brought you. Everything is flowing smoothly. Then, suddenly you receive distressing news that seems to suck the air out of you. What do you do now? What did Esther do?

The first thing that she did was come up with a rational excuse why she could not go to the king and plead with him for her Jewish people. "All the king's servants and the people of the king's provinces know that for any man or woman who comes to the king to the inner court who is not summoned, he has but one law, that he be put to death, unless the king holds out to him the golden scepter so that he may live. And I have not been summoned to come to the King for these thirty days" (Esther 4:11). It seems so much easier to come up with excuses to yourself and others of why you cannot use your blessings, your pull, your reputation, or your own life for such a strong purpose. These excuses can never fool God. He is the one who created you and put you into this position for His purpose.

God knows that exact words it will take to get you in line. When she told her cousin Mordecai this excuse, he told her some piercing words. "Then Mordecai told them to return this answer to Esther, Do not flatter yourself that you shall escape in the king's palace any more than all the other Jews. For if you keep silent at this time, relief and deliverance shall arise for the Jews from elsewhere, but you and your father's house will perish. And who knows but that you have come to the kingdom for such a time as this and for this very occasion?" (Esther 4:13–14, AMP). You must remember that God did not need you to carry out His divine purpose, but He did choose you right now for this time.

Therefore, Esther took a deep breath, took courage in God, and acted accordingly. She called a three-day fast for herself,

Courage Above Defeat

her servants, and all the Jews. She understood the importance of seeking God for direction in a time of distress. She planned to boldly go before the king, against their law, on behalf of her people even if it cost her life. Esther took courage.

JUST IN THE NICK OF TIME

On the third day of Esther's fast, she put on her royal clothes and went before the king. As soon as the king saw her, she obtained favor in his sight and he asked her what was bothering her. He also asked her what her request was. He offered her as much as half of his kingdom based on whatever she wanted. Prayer and fasting take care of the situation before you ever arrive there. When he saw her, he immediately was attentive to whatever she wanted. Normally, a person would be killed for coming before the king without his permission. Esther recognized that prayer and fasting were the key in overcoming all possible disasters. Do not ever think that just because you have money, success, a good husband, or a good life that you will have no need to pray and fast. No one is exempt from needing God. Remember, the same God that brought you here is the God that will keep you here.

Esther responded to the king by requesting that he and Haman come to a banquet that she prepared for them. He responded quickly to her request and brought Haman to the banquet. At this point, the king was very curious to know what Esther wanted. Because Esther sought the Lord before acting, she could rest assured that God was leading her. Likewise, as a woman of God, you must become Spirit-controlled in all that you do. Your decisions can affect the lives of others. It may not affect their physical lives like in Esther's case, but it can certainly affect their spiritual lives. When others see how blessed you are, you will become a role model. People will be watching your behavior and how you handle various circumstances. Be very careful where you go, what you say, and what you portray.

Single But Not Alone

At the banquet, the king asked her again what her request was. She requested that he and Haman come again to another banquet the following day and then she would reveal her request to him. King Ahasuerus was becoming more eager to find out what she desired. Meanwhile, Haman's pride overtook him. He thought these invitations from Esther were a sign of good standing with the king. However, he ran into Mordecai at the king's gate, and once again Mordecai refused to bow down and honor him. This angered him severely. When Haman told this to his wife and friends, they suggested that a seventy-foot gallows be built to hang Mordecai the next day.

As Haman arrived at the king's palace to speak to the king regarding hanging Mordecai, he received a very unexpected surprise. Just in the nick of time, the king commanded that Haman honor Mordecai in public for saving the king's life when He informed Esther about the two officials that plotted to kill the king. This humiliated Haman greatly. Once again, he complained about what had transpired to his wife and friends. While he was still talking with them, the king's servants came to bring him to Esther's banquet right way. Haman was planning to hang Mordecai this very day.

At the second banquet, the king eagerly asked Esther once again what her request was. Well, this time she told him all that Haman had plotted against her Jewish people. As a result, King Ahasuerus had Haman hanged on the same gallows that Haman intended to hang Mordecai on. The sequence of these events did not occur just by chance. God had a plan to save his people just in the nick of time. Why does God move just in the nick of time? This eliminates any possibility of concluding that anyone or anything brought this victory to past. Just in the nick of time enables God to receive the glory that only He deserves. God will bring you to a place of blessing and increase just in the nick of time to be a blessing and affect the destiny of others.

Courage Above Defeat

Medal of Courage

Queen Esther disclosed to the king that Mordecai was her cousin and Mordecai was promoted. She took courage and requested that something be written to revoke the documents that Haman had written to destroy the Jews on the thirteenth of the twelfth month. He granted her request and gave her and Mordecai the authority to do so. King Ahasuerus granted all the Jews the right to gather and defend themselves. This meant completely destroying anyone that might attack them on that day. These documents were sent out to all the people and became a law. When this day arrived, the Jews completely defeated all of their enemies with great triumph.

As a result, the Jews celebrate the fourteen and fifteenth days of this month annually as holidays because those were the days that they defeated their enemies. In order to keep these days remembered and spread throughout every generation, family, and city, Esther and Mordecai wrote another document confirming this celebration and recognition of these days. All of this was established at Esther's command. The bravery of one woman saved her people, made her cousin great, and established her name forever as a woman of courage and purpose.

Courage is intended not only for Esther, but for you also. God has brought you this far for a great purpose. Do not get sidetracked with the blessing and miss the window of opportunity to fulfill your God-given purpose. When you come face to face with the greatest challenge in your life, do not push it off, panic, or make rash decisions. Seek God first, wait for the answer, then act with boldness. Remember, this is only a setup. Your way of provision and favor will carry you through. Like Esther, your medal of courage awaits you.

CHAPTER 10

From Rags to Riches

WHEN WAS THE last time that you praised and honored God for how far you have come? Are you too blessed to remember where you were or how bad your circumstances were when Jesus found you? A woman that has been transformed from rags to riches must never lose sight of where God has brought her. This transformation did not occur by chance alone. It was the direct work of God. Whatever God touches must flourish from death to life, from darkness to light, from drought to rain, and from poverty to prosperity. After God has touched you, you can expect His riches to overtake you.

What does "from rags to riches" mean to you? Are you reminded of the Cinderella fairytale? This story describes how a young lady was transformed from a servant girl to royalty. The key to this story was her transformation from poverty to success. When Cinderella became a princess, there was no question of whether or not a change had occurred. This same young lady that had been ridiculed and neglected was now admired and well respected. In a similar respect, God intends for you to have riches in every area of your life. Riches extend to your finances, your health, your marriage, your family, and your eternal future. As a woman of God, you share in the inheritance of eternal riches:

> By having the eyes of your heart flooded with light, so that you can know and understand the hope to which He has called you, and how rich is His glorious inheritance in the saints (His set-apart ones), and [so that you can know and understand] what is the immeasurable and unlimited and surpassing greatness of His power in and for us who believe, as demonstrated in the working of His mighty strength.
> —Ephesians 1:18–19, amp

These riches are available to you, but serve no benefit if you are unaware that you have them. This lack of knowledge will keep you with a servant-girl mentality. That mentality revolves around thinking you will never get promoted, you will never get noticed, you will never get your business up and running, you will never get out of debt, and so forth. Many women have the misconception that getting married will change them from a servant-girl mentality to that of a queen. When God unites you with your husband, He makes you the queen of your household. Proverbs 12:4 states, "An excellent wife is the crown of her husband, but she who shames him is like rottenness in his bones." You cannot become the crown of your husband with a servant-girl mentality.

How do you go from rags to riches? First, you must change your way of thinking. This comes by accepting the fact that God has already given you access to unlimited wealth if you obey His Word. "Praise the Lord. Blessed is the man who fears the Lord, who finds great delight in his commands. His children will be mighty in the land; the generation of the upright will be blessed. Wealth and riches are in his house, and his righteousness endures forever" (Ps. 112:1–3, niv). Second, you must realize that God is the only One that can change

From Rags to Riches

your circumstances. "Who is like the Lord our God, who has His seat on high, who humbles Himself to regard the heavens and the earth! [The Lord] raises the poor out of dust and lifts the needy from the ash heap and the dung hill, that He may seat them with princes, even with the princes of His people" (Psalm 113:5–8, AMP).

Understanding and accepting God's truths and promises will carry you from a servant girl to a rich woman of mind, soul, and spirit. God desires for your divine destiny to be surrounded by supernatural prosperity. This final chapter anchors you to a place of divine wealth. We will discuss how you gain wealth from what you already have. You will learn how to put the right materials together to obtain unlimited riches. A woman of wealth will be your end result. Ladies, let us explore the final path to your true royalty.

STARTING ONLY WITH WHAT YOU HAVE

Every success story has a beginning. Someone began with a dream, idea, or goal. What appears to have been a small thought can later blossom into sheer success. There are different levels of success. These are financial, emotional, mental, and spiritual success. This society considers success to be the attainment of education, fame, money, or power. However, God shares a different view. "As for the rich in this world, charge them not to be proud and arrogant and contemptuous of others, not to set their hopes on uncertain riches, but on God, Who richly and ceaselessly provides us with everything for [our] enjoyment. [Charge them] to do good, to be rich in good works, to be liberal and generous of heart, ready to share [with others], in this way laying up for themselves [the riches that endure forever as] a good foundation for the future, so that they may grasp that which is life indeed" (1 Tim. 6:17–19, AMP).

In order to obtain true success, you must start with what you already have. Success begins on the inside of you then

Single But Not Alone

expresses itself outwardly. You do not have to wait for better circumstances to get successful results in your life. Instead, you must proceed by faith in God and obedience to His Word. God desires that you have financial success, but He expects you to do your part. We will discuss a woman who achieved financial success beginning with practically nothing:

> The wife of a man from the company of the prophets cried out to Elisha, "Your servant my husband is dead, and you know that he revered the LORD. But now his creditor is coming to take my two boys as his slaves." Elisha replied to her, "How can I help you? Tell me, what do you have in your house?" "Your servant has nothing there at all," she said, "except a little bottle of oil." Elisha said, "Go around and ask all your neighbors for empty jars. Don't ask for just a few. Then go inside and shut the door behind you and your sons. Pour oil into all the jars, and as each is filled, put it to one side." She left him and afterward shut the door behind her and her sons. They brought the jars to her and she kept pouring. When all the jars were full, she said to her son, "Bring me another one." But he replied, "There is not a jar left." Then the oil stopped flowing. She went and told the man of God, and he said, "Go, sell the oil and pay your debts. You and your sons can live on what is left."
> —2 KINGS 4:1–7, NIV

This widow took what she had and did with it as the man of God had instructed her. As a result, she no longer lived in lack. She could have elected not to do what he told her simply because it did not make logical sense. However, she was obedient and reaped the rewards as a result.

Emotional success manifests in the area of your feelings. This type of success is attained when you do not allow your emotions to control you. Your emotions change frequently and are undependable. God's Word does not depend on your

From Rags to Riches

emotions. Therefore, you cannot obey His Word through your emotions. You must obey His Word through your faith. Emotional success masters the fact that your present circumstances are subject to change if your actions remain consistent. Let's explore a woman who attained this type of success. Her name is Ruth:

> And when Boaz has eaten and drunk and his heart was merry, he went to lie down at the end of the heap of grain. Then [Ruth] came softly and uncovered his feet and lay down. At midnight the man was startled, and he turned over, and behold, a woman lay at his feet! And he said, Who are you? And she answered, I am Ruth your maidservant. Spread your wing [of protection] over your maidservant, for you are a next of kin. And he said, Blessed be you of the Lord, my daughter. For you have made this last loving-kindness greater than the former, for you have not gone after young men, whether poor or rich. And now, my daughter, fear not. I will do for you all you require, for all my people in the city know that you are a woman of strength (worth, bravery, capability).
> —RUTH 3:7–11, AMP

Ruth's circumstances appeared very grim. Her husband had died. She seemed to have lost everything. However, she chose to stay with her mother-in-law, Naomi, when neither of them had anything. She traveled with Naomi to a foreign country and served God. She did not allow her emotions to control her actions. Ruth did not become bitter, pursue relationships with men, or act in any way unbecomingly. Instead, she obeyed Naomi and focused on doing the things that were needed. Ruth was not on an emotional roller coaster. She remained consistent in her actions. Her emotional success gave her the courage to present herself to Boaz to make her request. As a result, they later married and had a child named Obed. Jesus was a descendant from this bloodline.

Mental success is attained when you master your thought processes. Many thoughts may enter your mind, but you have the ability to cast them down. "(For the weapons of our warfare are not carnal, but mighty through God to the pulling down of strong holds;) Casting down imaginations, and every high thing that exalteth itself against the knowledge of God, and bringing into captivity every thought to the obedience of Christ" (2 Cor. 10:4–5, KJV). When you allow your thoughts to take possession over you, you lose the ability to focus on what is truly important. "For the rest, brethren, whatever is true, whatever is worthy of reverence and is honorable and seemly, whatever is just, whatever is pure, whatever is lovely and lovable, whatever is kind and winsome and gracious, if there is any virtue and excellence, if there is anything worthy of praise, think on and weigh and take account of these things [fix your minds on them]" (Phil. 4:8, AMP).

Mental success will keep your motives pure. It will prevent you from yielding to jealousy and selfishness. "Make my joy complete by being of the same mind, maintaining the same love, united in spirit, intent on one purpose. Do nothing from selfishness or empty conceit, but with humility of mind regard one another as more important than yourselves; do not merely look out for your own personal interests, but also for the interests of others" (Phil. 2:2–4). Controlling your thoughts will enable God's peace to envelop your mind as you maintain a continuous rest.

Spiritual success develops out of spiritual growth. Spiritual success will manifest as you continue to soar in new levels of faith. Faith relies completely on God. It gives you full security in God. Security means freedom from doubt, anxiety, or fear. It is sheer confidence in God. "Truly I tell you, whoever says to this mountain, Be lifted up and thrown into the sea! and does not doubt at all in his heart but believes that what he says will take place, it will be done for him. For this reason I am telling you, whatever you ask for in prayer, believe (trust and be confident) that it is granted to you, and you will [get it]" (Mark 11:23–24, AMP). Spiritual success results when your prayer life and your faith unite to elicit complete security in God's Word.

He wants you to succeed spiritually because it draws you closer to Him. When you become closer to God, trust develops. Spiritual success is not dependent on past mistakes but on present faith. "Now faith is the substance of things hoped for, the evidence of things not seen" (Heb. 11:1, KJV). Although you are not perfect, your faith in God can be perfected. "[And we] continue to pray especially and with most intense earnestness night and day that we may see you face to face and mend and make good whatever may be imperfect and lacking in your faith" (1 Thess. 3:10, AMP). Perfected faith gives the power to declare great things from God to change your life and the world around you for His kingdom.

ALL OF THE RIGHT MATERIALS

The greatest asset to an empire is the foundation upon which it is built. It must be built with the right materials in order to stand under all conditions over time. While your successes are being established, God can begin structuring out your divine empire. The problem with many people is that they want God to move before they begin achieving success in those areas. These people are lacking the right materials. Successful people do their part to enable God to do His part. Jesus Christ is their role model and promoter. He needs the right materials to build on. He desires to make you His protégé. This is a woman whose training, welfare, or career is promoted by Christ Himself. After all, He is the head of the church. He has all power and authority. He certainly has the right credentials to train you.

You do not need to have your personal success plan all figured out before God can move on your behalf. As you allow God to achieve those areas of success in your life, they will fit into His higher plan your life. His plan greatly exceeds yours. "For My thoughts are not your thoughts, neither are your ways My ways, says the Lord. For as the heavens are higher than the earth, so are My ways higher than your ways and My thoughts than your thoughts" (Isa. 55:8–9, AMP). God is a creator. He creates ways to promote you. You must take what you have and allow God to put it together for this to work. This is where giving becomes so important. When you give to God without restraints, He gives to you without restraints. God takes pleasure when you prosper. "Let them shout for joy, and be glad, that favour my righteous cause: yea, let them say continually, Let the LORD be magnified, which hath pleasure in the prosperity of his servant" (Ps. 35:27, KJV).

It is important not to confuse earthly wealth with God's prosperity. God is certainly able to prosper you with money. However, there are ungodly people that have large sums of money, but do not have God's prosperity. They may not have peace in their minds, rest for their souls, healing in their bodies, or emotional stability. On the other hand, God's prosperity entitles you to everything when you obey His laws on giving. God does not expect more from you than what He was willing to give on your behalf. "For God so greatly loved and dearly prized the world that He [even] gave up His only begotten (unique) Son, so that whoever believes in (trusts in, clings to, relies on) Him shall not perish (come to destruction, be lost) but have eternal (everlasting) life" (John 3:16, AMP).

God gave His only Son because He loved so deeply. He wants you successful so that you can give and minister to others in order that His Gospel is preached across the world. He expects you to give cheerfully:

> Remember this: Whoever sows sparingly will also reap sparingly, and whoever sows generously will also reap generously. Each man should give what he had decided in his heart to give, not reluctantly or under compulsion,

From Rags to Riches

for God loves a cheerful giver. And God is able to make all grace abound to you, so that in all things at all times, having all that you need, you will abound in every good work. As it is written: He has scattered abroad his gifts to the poor; his righteousness endures forever. Now he who supplies seed to the sower and bread for food will also supply and increase your store of seed and will enlarge the harvest of your righteousness. You will be made rich in every way so that you can be generous on every occasion, and through us your generosity will result in thanksgiving to God.

—2 Corinthians 9:6–11, niv

The previous scripture stresses that if you give, you will be made rich in every way. The more you give, the more that you are blessed to give more. This process is constant. Giving is not limited to just money. It is giving of your time, your efforts, and other your resources in order to serve others. If you do so, you will reap more than you have ever thought possible. When you give to God through your local church it enables the church to continue. If you do not give to your local church, you are actually robbing God.

"Will a man rob God? Yet you rob me. But you ask, 'How do we rob you?' In tithes and offerings. You are under a curse—the whole nation of you—because you are robbing me. Bring the whole tithe into the storehouse, that there may be food in my house. Test me in this," says the Lord Almighty, "and see if I will not throw open the floodgates of heaven and pour out so much blessing that you will not have room enough for it."

—Malachi 3:8–10, niv

It is clear that God commands you to give. He expects you to be obedient and act accordingly. You have everything to gain if you are obedient and everything to lose if you are disobedient.

Single But Not Alone

The choice is yours. You have come too far to lose now. Take hold of these materials and allow God to work through you to accumulate this wealth from above. "Instruct them to do good, to be rich in good works, to be generous and ready to share, storing up for themselves the treasure of a good foundation for the future, so that they may take hold of that which is life indeed" (1 Tim. 6:18-19). Remember, that your work will not be in vain. The rewards will last from now to eternity.

Unlimited Riches

What do you think attracts people to all-you-can-eat buffets or unlimited long-distance telephone plans? Neither of them have limitations. After you have paid the price for the buffet or telephone plan, you are then entitled to what you paid for. Jesus Christ paid a high price for you on Calvary to bring you into unlimited riches. "And [so that you can know and understand] what is the immeasurable and unlimited and surpassing greatness of His power in and for us who believe, as demonstrated in the working of His mighty strength, which He exerted in Christ when He raised Him from the dead and seated Him at His [own] right hand in the heavenly [places]" (Eph. 1:19-20, AMP). There are no limits to God's power. He did not raise up Christ only, but you also. "And He raised us up together with Him and made us sit down together [giving us joint seating with Him] in the heavenly sphere [by virtue of our being] in Christ Jesus (the Messiah, the Anointed One)" (Eph. 2:6, AMP).

So what does this entitle you to? Unlimited riches! The only limitations that you have are the ones that you have set for yourself. God does not have any so why should you? After all, you have been raised up with Jesus Christ in heavenly places. This means that you are part of a supreme royal family. Any loving father wants to shower his daughter with blessings. It is your heavenly Father's pleasure to give you good things when

From Rags to Riches

He is placed first in your life. "Only aim at and strive for and seek His kingdom, and all these things shall be supplied to you also. Do not be seized with alarm and struck with fear, little flock, for it is your Father's good pleasure to give you the kingdom!" (Luke 12:31–32, AMP). God is not trying to withhold good things from you. On the contrary, He is trying to get good things to you. "No good thing will he withhold from them that walk uprightly" (Ps. 84:11, KJV).

The upright inherit unlimited riches. These are people that are in right standing with God. They shun evil and cling to what is good. In short, they follow God's commandments. "Blessed and fortunate and happy and spiritually prosperous (in that state in which the born-again child of God enjoys His favor and salvation) are those who hunger and thirst for righteousness (uprightness and right standing with God), for they shall be completely satisfied!" (Matt 5:6, AMP). There is certainly a connection with living right, favor, and prosperity. It seems so easy that everyone should desire to live this way. However, when sin entered the world as a result of Adam's fall, the natural man struggled with the spiritual man in walking before God. However, because Christ became the second Adam, He broke through the curse of sin and made a way for you to become righteous in God through Christ.

You have been made rich in righteousness. This gives you the access to tap into the windows of heaven. Do not expect everyone to be excited for you. Actually, you will face persecution. "Blessed and happy and enviably fortunate and spiritually prosperous (in the state in which the born-again child of God enjoys and find satisfaction in God's favor and salvation, regardless of his outward conditions) are those who are persecuted for righteousness' sake (for being and doing right), for theirs is the kingdom of heaven!" (Matt. 5:10, AMP). You will be blessed despite the personal attacks and criticism of others because you are upright with God. No person, economy, or any calamity can limit the source of your riches.

Single But Not Alone

Your riches will actually be a testimony of what God has done for you. "Meanwhile a large crowd of Jews found out that Jesus was there and came, not only because of him but also to see Lazarus, whom he had raised from the dead" (John 12:9, NIV). You can win people over to Christ through your testimony of what He did for you. Many people may not accept Christ until they see Him through the lives of others. Keep in mind that you are on a journey to live out your God-given destiny. There is a purpose for your riches. God must receive the glory for it. Keep a thankful, merry heart, always remembering that true riches come from above.

A Woman of Wealth

A wealthy woman is one who lives in the presence of God. Her wealth is manifested by the glory of God in and around her. The glory of God is His manifested presence. This glory radiates outwardly when Christ is inside of you. "To whom God would make known what is the riches of the glory of this mystery of among the Gentiles; which is Christ in you, the hope of glory" (Col. 1:27, KJV). By faith, you can take hold of this powerful revelation of the glory that shines from within you. Picture in your mind the appearance of a queen as she makes an entrance. You probably imagine fine clothing, a beautiful diamond crown, and an array of precious sparkling jewels. When you are a woman of wealth, this is only a glimpse of how others see the glory of God upon you.

The jewels of a woman go far beyond her jewelry. God revealed to me the representation of His glory within and around a woman through gems. The diamond stretches forth above her head. A sapphire, emerald, and ruby circle her inner core. As they rotate, they become so intertwined that they can no longer be differentiated. The diamond represents holiness, purity, godliness, and righteousness. The sapphire represents peace, coolness, calmness, rest, and serenity. The emerald rep-

From Rags to Riches

resents power, prosperity, riches, and wealth. The ruby represents salvation through the blood, sanctification, perfection, cleanliness, and justification. Ezekiel had several visions of God's glory. This is how he describes one encounter:

> Over the head of the [combined] living creature there was the likeness of a firmament, looking like the terrible and awesome [dazzling of shining] crystal or ice stretched across the expanse of sky over their heads. And above the firmament that was over their heads was the likeness of a throne in appearance like a sapphire stone, and seated above the likeness of a throne was a likeness with the appearance of a Man. From what had the appearance of His waist upward, I saw a luster as it were glowing metal with the appearance of fire enclosed round about within it; and from the appearance of His waist downward, I saw as it were the appearance of fire, and there was brightness [of a halo] round about Him.
> —Ezekiel 1:22, 26–27, AMP

This "likeness with appearance of a Man" was Jesus Christ. He was all God, but humbled himself to the form a man and died on the cross for you. Through this, He brought you into union with Himself. As a woman of wealth, you also have a part in His glory. Brightness will shine all around you. This will attract a lost and dying world to the glory that awaits them.

Epilogue

YOUR JOURNEY BEGAN as single woman in search of her destiny. You have now discovered the keys to becoming a woman of excellence in every area of your life. This book is intended to be a framework to guide you into a life-long journey. The truths in this book will have lasting effects whether you are single or married. It is now your time to watch your divine destiny unfold right before your eyes. God will never fail you. He already knows your every desire. My single sister, be bold, be strong, and journey on. It will come to pass.

To Contact the Author

Diane Sims
P.O. Box 19174
Lenexa, KS 66285-9174

www.dianesims.com